Compass Rose

Compass Rose

Carly Eccles Sheaffer

To request permissions, contact the publisher at contact@boundtobrew.com

Library of Congress Cataloging-in-Publication Data has been applied for.

ISBN 978-1-953500-02-1

First Edition

Edited by Pauline Harris and Danielle Manahan

Printed by Steuben Press in USA

Team Publishing
9457 S University Blvd. 819 Highlands Ranch, CO 80126

Boundtobrew.com

To Dad, who always found the roses, who taught us why they matter.

To Mom, who has listened to and loved us through every part of our journey.

To both, for teaching us to find our story.

To Sheaff, who is the point on my compass that always leads to home.

To Adalyn, Bria and Bryce, who always find the magic.

I would like to thank the Bound to Brew team: Chris and Ethan, for believing in this story and finding its place in the world. I'd also like to thank the editors and staff at Bound to Brew who worked hard to make this the best version it could be. Thank you to my dearest friends who have cheered my writing on; thank you to my peer-reviewers Kristen and Casey, who told me to go for it, reading the roughest parts and sending comments, suggestions, questions to make it better, deeper, more real. Thank you to my brothers and sisters – blood and beyond – who were my strongest cheerleaders. To all my family who has given me such love, faith, and support. Thank you to Mom, who years ago helped me record notes of Dad's stories of the roses, who has read every piece of writing I've thrown her way, who is our own version of Charlotte. Thank you to Dad, our constant, who faithfully told of the roses, who taught me what dad-daughter warmth is all about it, and who showed us what moments truly matter. I have such deep gratitude and love for Grandma and Grandad and the house piled in with family on Priscilla Lane; the memories we all carry with us, from roses to croquet to patio-rocking… they remind us that you are both always with us, just like the roses. And thank you to my husband Sheaff, my other half, who believed in me during the highs, the lows, and all the moments in between, who has been ignored countless times during writing and editing but loves me anyway.

Our village is deep and wide and filled with the best people in the world.

CONTENTS

PART I

He was speechless as he stared into a face he had sworn ten years ago he would never see again. They say time freezes, but he could hear every tick of the clock on the wall behind them; it seemed absurdly loud, the only sound in the room. In every passing second, he reached, but failed, to grasp a thought, a word, a question to voice out loud.

The woman in front of him blinked twice. "I ..." She faltered. "I thought you were dead," Annie finally said simply, her unreserved shock covering every other emotion that surged beneath the surface.

"You what?" he said stupidly, his eyes not moving from her face, a face he had loved with every fiber of his soul for years.

"The car accident. Months after I left. I heard about it. I read the article; it said you were dead." Her voice broke on the last word. Her eyes scanned him, as if convincing herself that Shaun, the man who had almost proposed to her years ago, was truly in front of her now.

"The car accident ..." He struggled to regain his thought process. Images flipped through his mind, like the toy camera he'd had growing up. Look through the lens, click the button, a new picture appears. *Click.* Headlights. *Click.* The white of the airbag. *Click.* The crushed metal of the hood, folded up like a crumpled blanket. "The reporter got the story wrong; the paper did ... There was a correction later ..." He stopped, at a loss for more of an explanation. There was no simple way to continue.

Annie blew out her breath, shaking her head. She reached out, like she was going to touch him, then pulled back. "You're alive," she whispered, almost to herself. "And you're here. What are you doing here, Shaun?"

His name being spoken aloud by her brought him slightly out of his stunned daze. Realizing he did not know the answer to her question, he turned to his small daughter, who was standing next to him, intently looking up at the two adults as though their reunion was nothing out of the ordinary. She had a hint of a smile on her face.

Annie followed his gaze to the child, and then looked back at Shaun, her eyes questioning. He lowered himself down to his daughter until their faces were level.

She met his eyes and grinned, as though she knew the greatest secret in the world. Her small fingers came up and pointed to the rose painted on the sign that hung on the wall behind the counter.

"I knew we would find something special here," she said. "All I had to do was follow the roses."

Chapter 2

The garden, much like his daughter, was one of the few patches of happiness in Shaun's world. Where he had felt gray and worn within, he now felt surprising lifts of color and energy and life digging in the dirt, moving the little rectangle of earth that was his own.

The second week after moving into a small, grungy house that was nonetheless an improvement from the apartment they had lived in for the last five years, he used a Saturday to turn the tiny backyard into the beginnings of a rose garden.

Olivia stepped out onto the porch in her waitressing uniform, letting the battered screen door slam behind her. "What are you doing?" she demanded. A familiar, tired annoyance sat on her lip.

She had not lost all of the prettiness that had attracted him to her seven years ago, leaning across a pancake house counter. Her smile had been a solace after he had left his hometown, running from mistakes and ghosts and other hauntings that felt heavier whenever he stayed still. Olivia had put the chocolate chips in his pancakes in the shape of a smiley-face—something she would never do now. She had a beautiful, wide smile that made her dark brown eyes shrink into happy half-moons, but he hadn't seen it in months. His fault, he knew. Her once-soft skin bagged under her eyes and drooped with the exhaustion of long hours and many cigarettes. Her brown hair was shorter now, cropped across her angular face to yield a stylish look. It had only been seven years since she had told him about the positive pregnancy tests, head in her hands, like the air had gone out of her.

Shaun had given her space to decide but promised if they kept the baby that he wouldn't leave them, something Olivia had seen males do over and over since high school. He would be there, formulating a plan, figuring out how to take care of them both. They agreed to stay together, at least until the baby was older. Childcare was so expensive that they worked out a schedule that would allow one of them to stay home with her. Olivia worked afternoons and nights dishing meals out at the local diner, while he worked opposite hours on odd jobs where he could make his own hours, leaving early in the morning so that he could be back in time for Olivia to get to work. Money was tight, but he wouldn't trade those days and hours with his daughter for anything.

He was the one who chose her name: Marie. He was the one who fed her with a warm bottle in the middle of the night, walked her in endless circles around the small apartment when she cried, changed her diapers, scratched out her milestones in a spiral notebook he kept in a desk drawer. He took and collected photos of Marie, swaddled on her first day home from the hospital. Marie drooling in her faithful bouncer where she babbled and played her early days. Sleeping, butt up, knees tucked in the second-hand crib he refinished for her. Her first food. Her first steps. Her first time visiting a zoo, in love with the elephants. Her first tricycle, which she rode in endless circles in an old parking lot. He kept all of these and little scraps of memories in a wooden box he specially made, saving them for himself and he wasn't sure who else.

The cost of living in the city was high, but they had saved up enough to rent a small cheap house in a better neighborhood when Marie turned six. It had a kitchen, a bathroom, one bedroom where they slept, with Marie on a trundle bed beside them, and a small open space with a couch and television that some people might claim was a family room. They had virtually no front yard, but they did have a small plot in the back where Shaun sat now, planting another small rose bush that would be blooming soon.

"What are you doing?" Olivia questioned him again impatiently when he did not respond right away.

"I'm planting a rose garden," he answered. When she stared at him for further explanation, he shrugged and answered honestly, "My dad loved roses. I guess I want my family to love them too."

Olivia shook her head, the quiet listening moments from their early days of dating long in the past. She shrugged back at him. "Your father is gone, Shaun. Our 'family' was a mistake from a stupid night of not being careful enough. I don't think roses are going to be our happily ever after."

Shaun stopped shoveling, staring at Olivia. She just wanted a fight; he struggled not to bite the bait. She turned to walk back inside, then turned around. "Our plumbing is off again; I have to leave for work in five minutes. Marie spilt milk all over the rug, which is going to stink like hell if we forget about it again. The car needs work done, and you're out here planting a garden like that's what matters." She shook her head in disgust and turned to walk back through the door. Marie was just scooting outside with her kindergarten workbook in her skinny arms. Olivia held the door open for her apathetically.

"Are you going to work, Mommy?" Marie asked, looking up at her mother.

"Yeah, I'll be back tonight sometime, hun," Olivia said flatly. "Shaun ..."

He looked up from the hole he had gone back to breaking, sorting through the rocks of the soil.

"Do something useful with yourself, would you?" The screen door slammed behind her.

Marie watched her mother retreat. She loved the pink outfit Olivia wore with the black apron and wondered why she didn't smile more in it. One time, she put the dress on like she was playing dress-up at school and began bringing dishes out to her parents, serving them invisible pancakes and make-believe orange juice. Her dad laughed and gobbled them up, but her mom told her to take it off and God help her if she ever learned what it was like to wear it for a living. Marie didn't try on the dress anymore.

"Whatcha' doing, Daddy?"

"What does it look like I'm doing, goof?" he teased, poking her stomach gently.

She grinned and picked up a shovel to help him dig. "Planting flowers? Can I help? Will they be pretty?"

He eyed her book, which she wished she had left inside now. "Before you help, let's work on those letters. Then I'll tell you all about the flowers." He picked up the book she had set down and asked her what she was learning.

"Vowels! *A. E. I. O. U.* And sometimes *Y!*" she said knowledgeably.

"Smart girl! What vowel is in 'rose'?" he challenged, pointing at the bushes beside them.

She mouthed the word and bit her lip, thinking. It seemed like an easy one. Not much was easy about reading for her yet, as the sounds took so long for her brain to put together, but it was at least more fun with her dad.

Shaun looked at her, taking in her concentration, watching her face. Her skin was like his, ruddy and freckled. She had thick hair pulled back with a headband, although it was a dark brown like Olivia's, not his reddish-blond. She had his same deep blue eyes and a dimple buried in her left cheek. She was small for her age and sat criss-cross applesauce on the ground beside him, leaning her soft weight against his large shoulder.

"Hmmm," she said out loud, tapping her chin. "O? Roooose."

He nodded. "You got it! Now write 'rose' in the dirt here for me." When she looked dubiously at him, he nudged her encouragingly. "Sure you can; sound it out … What does it start with?"

"*Rrrrr*, rrrrose. *Rrr* is *R*," she said, picking up the stick to try writing again. She began to write the letter backward, but Shaun wiped it away.

She giggled and wrote it the correct way. "Rrrrooose … *O* comes next." She drew her circle again quickly, imitating the shape of her mouth like Shaun had taught her.

"Rossssse. *Ssss* is S," she said.

"S is like ssssnake," Shaun explained, drawing it for her. "Exactly—all curvy, just like one is slithering by you." He wiped it away and gave her back the stick so she could try.

"Now, what?" she asked.

"You put an *E* on the end." The pair sat and looked at their work of art. The letters were quaintly childish, scratched out in the dirt beside their rose garden.

"Tell me about the flowers, Daddy," Marie said, ready for her reward.

Shaun smiled despite the hollow feeling that sank into his stomach every time he mentioned his father. "Well my dad, your grandad, he loved roses. He knew how to grow the most beautiful, amazing roses you've ever seen. Yellow ones, red ones, pink, white … you name it. You'll see them really soon when they grow and bloom. You can help me water them every day after school if you want." Shaun helped Marie brush the leaves of the rose bush gently.

"Flowers need a lot of care to be pretty. It's almost like having a baby that you have to look after all the time."

"Feed them and protect them and stuff?" Marie said, her head cocked to one side. "My teacher said you can even sing Beyoncé to plants, and they grow better."

Shaun laughed. "Sure, Beyoncé is great for flowers. And you've got to feed and fertilize and water them. See those two bushes over there? Those are white ones, and they're the hardest to grow. You have to be really careful, because this fungus called the black spot will come and make them sick, or this nasty little bug called a Japanese beetle will come and eat the petals and roses."

Marie made a face then changed the subject, attention span short as ever. "What's Grandad like?"

"Well," Shaun began, taking a deep breath. Questions were endless from Marie since the day she knew how to ask them. And sometimes, her questions were the only link connecting him to the past, at least the only link he wanted. It was a strange paradox of distance and a child's simple love that made it safe to talk to her.

"He was from England, which is a country all the way across the ocean, so he talked like this," he said, putting on a British accent, which made Marie giggle.

"His name was Jerry Murray. He was always very calm and never got upset. Really gentle, you know? It was hard to have a problem with him. And he loved to grow roses. He had us go out every Saturday to work in the garden, weeding around the flowers to make sure the soil was broken off so the water could get to them and help them grow. He was so proud of those gardens, would always cut roses on Sunday and bring them to the table for Sunday dinner."

"Can we do that?" Marie tried to picture a vaseful of roses on their card table in the kitchen.

"Of course we can."

"What else?" she prodded.

8

"What else ..." Shaun sighed, leaning back against the brick wall, picking the dirt out from underneath his nails. Marie flopped back and imitated him, crossing her legs just as he did. "He saw yard work as education, or school, just like your kindergarten, only it was all about gardening. He loved to explain the best place to prune, how you should nurture the plants, how much fertilizer to use, all those different jobs. But our favorite job was getting rid of the beetles. Our neighbor, Mr. Summers, would break their heads off."

"Ew!" Marie cut in, making a face.

Shaun laughed. "Yeah, we couldn't do that. It was way too gross. So your grandad gave us a mayonnaise jar full of gasoline, and we would drop them in there. We used to have contests on who could find the most beetles." Shaun was now talking fluidly, not aware of the city around him, completely immersed in his memories. Marie listened, resting easily against her dad as his deep voice rolled on.

"We always worked on roses Saturday mornings, right after cartoons. Cartoons were only an hour, and there was no football, no fishing, no playing until the roses were taken care of. And the worst was, when we finally could play football, sometimes a wild ball would fall into a bush and break it. We got in trouble, and then we were always having to pool our money to buy a new football after one got popped from the thorns."

Marie laughed at the thought of her dad in trouble. "How many bushes were there?" she asked, trying to picture it.

"Grandad had over seventy-five rose bushes in our backyard." Shaun smiled as Marie's mouth dropped, looking at their meager collection of five rose bushes that filled their small plot.

"Wow." She paused and eyed her dad. She knew other kids had grandparents around; plenty picked up her friends in carpools, and there had even been a grandparent lunch at school one day. Her teacher had sat beside her, but it didn't quite fill the empty space she felt. When she asked her mom and dad, they said sometimes people's grandparents lived far away or had died, and they changed the subject. "Why doesn't Grandad come to visit us?" Marie asked tentatively.

Shaun closed his eyes for a moment before he answered. "Well, Grandad died before you were even born." He gave a sad little half-smile. "So he can only visit us through things like the roses."

"Through the roses?"

"Roses are a sign of Grandad. After he died, we put a bouquet of roses from his garden where we buried him." He swallowed and shifted, barely able to recall that day without a heaviness seizing his chest. "Then, during the next few years, roses kept turning up in odd places. I'd be walking through the woods in December and find a rose growing somewhere totally unexpected. Roses bloomed if I was feeling sad and missed him, or in seasons other than when they were supposed to. It was like a sign from Grandad that he was with us. A rose even bloomed right outside our window when you were born." Shaun's eyes glistened briefly, remembering. "It made me feel like he was there, smiling right at you."

Marie smiled at this. Then she asked, "Did Mama know him?"

Shaun shook his head. Marie started to ask why, but Shaun was already cleaning up his tools, and he told her to go in and wash up. "That's enough stories for today." As he washed the dirt from his hands and put the garden tools back, he let his mind close up the box of thoughts about his past again. Leaving it open was too hard.

**

10

There was a lot in the world that Olivia hated. But none so much as that look Shaun gave her.

She had gotten used to disliking things, dismissing them, shrugging off any large emotions with a distaste for anything bright and sunny and joyful. Her dislike festered until it turned into an unfortunate combination of apathy and bitterness. And that is what she felt every time Shaun looked at her like that.

He didn't used to. His face didn't used to be so resigned or tired. He used to look her up and down when they would go to the bar and sit for hours, drinking and laughing. They had one rule: No questions about the past. They never did anything too serious, and most of it went into the late hours of the night. But Shaun had a certain kindness about him that Olivia wasn't used to, a sort of thoughtfulness that didn't seem unusual to him. He remembered her favorite foods. He asked about small details of her day, remembered things she had casually mentioned. He fixed anything that was broken around the house, made it nicer. He kissed her on the forehead once; the gesture was strangely foreign.

But neither of them was ready for a baby. She took five tests, each little line showing up bolder than the one before. She almost went to the clinic without telling him, but she knew that wasn't fair, not to someone like him.

"You … you can't be pregnant," he stuttered.

"Well, I am. I'm beyond late, and the test came back positive. I've been to the doctor, and I'm two months gone," she said matter-of-factly. No hint of sparkle hid in her eyes; there was no sense of joy. Only a flat acceptance. She knew the nights of drinking, laughing, and cab rides home were done. She knew the playful dating, and sex, and the freeness they gave each other were gone. All the good they brought to each other—it was all done. And in its place, obligation.

She'd seen a pamphlet for postpartum depression one time. But that wasn't it. She didn't feel sad. On the surface she felt numb, and underneath, a quiet anger chafed at what little relationship they'd started with. The distance grew. And now, she hated that look Shaun gave her, one not of regret, but of resignation. He was settling for her. She knew he was. He never looked at Marie that way. No, the looks he saved for his daughter were of pride and love. She remembered when Marie was born his eyes watered over, the tear lines mixing into his beard. He carried an all-consuming worry for everything about her. How much she ate, how much she slept, if she was breathing in her crib. Sure, he lost his patience with her and got annoyed with her tantrums or when she didn't listen, but Olivia knew she would never get that look of simple love he had for Marie. Marie filled Shaun up with something that was shiny and bright. For Olivia, motherhood didn't come as easily.

Olivia didn't know how to be a good mom. She never had one, at least not that she could remember clearly. Bits and pieces, maybe. She vaguely remembered listening to her mom read her a book about the little engine that could, leaning against her hard side while her mom rubbed her back. That was the best memory she could recall. She remembered burnt fish sticks for dinner, her mom swearing as the oven smoked. She remembered her voice was always impatient, always angry. She remembered waiting for her to come back, waiting, waiting, waiting. Those memories left a searing pain that never quite left her chest, knowing her mother didn't love her enough to stay.

Olivia tried to soothe Marie a few times after she was born, but she just kept crying. Shaun was always better at making Marie happy, so Olivia eventually relied on him to do so. Disappointment was no stranger to Olivia. Rather than stare in its face again, she decided to set the standard low. And lower, and lower. Sometimes she wanted to leave too, completely abandon Shaun and Marie and the looks they gave her. She glanced down at her hand; people used to look at it all the time when she was pregnant. There was no ring. No real family. She wouldn't leave her little girl, not like her mom did. But she felt stuck, resentful, hopeless. Olivia cracked open a cheap beer and sipped on it in silence until the bus's brakes squeaked in with their heavy greeting that said, "This is your life now."

Chapter 3

That Monday, Marie got off the school bus at the top of her street and found a travel company brochure blown up against the fence. The bright yellow on the front caught her eye, and she grabbed it before another gust of wind blew it away. She carefully opened the front, and her mouth dropped at the pictures that lay before her. It had been designed to fit a great deal of information on one piece of paper, so by the time she unfolded it completely, she was holding a paper the size of a pillowcase in her hands. Glossy pictures danced across the page. Pictures of white beaches with crystal blue oceans; green mountains looming massively on the horizon; castles aged thousands of years in the middle of the countryside; a neat pavement path weaving its way through an autumn forest of bright orange, yellow, and red leaves; a man dressed in amazingly vivid colors beating on a drum, his skin the color of her father's coffee; the sandy-colored desert stretching lazily across a hilly terrain, yielding nothing but a smooth surface that met with a clear blue sky. Marie was in awe.

"Daddy! Daddy!" she cried, rushing into her house with the brochure tight in hand.

"He's not here," her mom answered. Marie found her sitting at the small table Shaun had crafted for dinners. Bills were piled in front of her, a beer in one hand and smoke curling from a cigarette in the other. "I got off work early, so he went to do some extra shifts painting." Her words slurred more than usual together, and her gaze did not follow Marie very clearly. "Go do your homework or something." She stumbled up from the table and turned on the television, not looking at Marie anymore.

Marie knew to avoid Olivia, staying in the bedroom quietly as to not disturb her mother. She waited until Shaun got home that evening, passing time with the small corner of toys—treasures she and Shaun had found at yard sales. She even colored a picture of all the vowels to show Shaun when he got home. She waited until she heard his footsteps at the door, and upon recognizing them, she jumped up from her trundle bed to see him. She was standing in the bedroom doorway when she heard Olivia snap at him about slamming the door. The sound hurt her head.

"What are you doing?" Shaun said in surprise, taking in Olivia's state. He looked at his watch. "It's like, 4:45. How long ..." he trailed off, his surprise fading quickly into frustration.

"Almost happy hour, right?" she snickered. Her hand formed the "rock out" symbol, waving lazily from the couch.

"That's not funny." His voice lowered dangerously. "You've got a six-year-old daughter in the house to take care of. God, Olivia, you're not eighteen anymore."

"Yeah, I'm twenty-seven and living the life, Shaun. A kid and her father and a minimum-wage job serving people who barely look at me. Like this is the dream? You want to get drunk too, baby?" Her thin arm swayed in the air. Shaun knew this was her at her worst. "Oh, maybe we can have another. Make our life even better." She tried to wave him out of the way to turn her attention back to the TV, but he shut it off angrily.

"Where's Marie?" he asked through clenched teeth.

"In the bedroom," she said, nodding her head half-heartedly in that direction. "Don't worry … not hard to find … there's only one."

Marie drew back behind the door so they wouldn't see her listening. Through the crack in the door, she saw Shaun bend down and pick Olivia's small frame up, as though she didn't weigh more than a few pounds.

"What the hell are you doing?" she swung at him but missed by far. "Put me down!"

"Hush," he said, and took her into the bathroom and closed the door, hoping to hide the fight as much as possible from Marie. He set Olivia down gently in the tub and turned the shower on full blast at the coldest possible temperature.

A slur of swear words sputtered out of her as the water blasted on her. "Shit, Shaun!" She tried to hold her hand against the water, but it sprayed heavily on her, drowning out her words. Shaun could see right through her thin tank top but took her chin firmly in his hands after shutting off the water. She shook her head, droplets flying from her chin-length hair, mascara running down her high cheekbones.

"Listen to me," he said quietly and fiercely. "I know you don't like this life. It's not what I pictured either. But we have got ourselves a daughter who does not deserve to hear crap like this. Do you understand what I'm saying? She is *six years old*, Olivia. You don't have to love me; I'm not asking you to do that. But for God's sake, love her enough to spare her from this. You cannot get drunk in the afternoon and take care of your child, you got it? You cannot do that to her."

Olivia glared into those blue eyes she once found so captivating but now only tortured her. "I got it," she said defiantly, shoving his hands off her face.

"No," he glowered down at her, taking her wrists in his strong hands, which were covered in blotches of white paint.

16

"You want to be angry at me; that's fine. You want to be unhappy with yourself; that's fine. But do not drink it off, and do *not* let it out on Marie. Do not."

She glared at the wall as he let go of her wrists and laid her arms on her lap. The room, along with the words he had spoken, spun around her with such intensity that she dared not respond.

"Don't come out of here until you're sober," he said, closing the door behind him.

Marie was still behind the door when Shaun stepped into the room.

"Hey, sweetie," Shaun said, reaching out to pick her up and set her on his lap. "Why were you behind the door?"

"Were you and Mommy fighting about me?" she asked, chewing on a loose strand of hair near her chin.

Shaun's eyes darted toward the door, which remained closed. "Not about you at all. Just about Mama's work."

Marie nodded; her dad had taken her to a pancake house once and told her about her mother's old job there, and how she used to put chocolate chips in the pancakes. Not only that, but she made them into smiley faces. Marie loved imagining her mom working in her pretty outfit there, making smiling pancakes for Shaun.

"Did you work any on the rose garden today?" she asked, thinking about things that made her dad happy.

"Sure did! There's just enough light out for you to see … I made and painted a trestle at work too, so they'll have something to hold onto besides that old metal fence when they start to grow." He took her hand, and they walked past the closed bathroom door to the backyard where Marie saw a beautiful white trestle set up against the metal fence.

"Ooooh! Daddy! It's so pretty!" She clapped her hands in delight and jumped up to give him a hug. He smiled and lifted her up.

17

"Now, missy, tell me about your day. Did you turn in your homework?"

She nodded and ran to get her book to show him the big sticker on the top of her page. She also grabbed the brochure and stuck it under the book, so when he set her schoolwork down, he found he was holding her newfound treasure.

"Well, well, well, what is this?" he asked, turning the brightly colored pamphlet over. "You planning a trip, sweetie?"

She pointed to the pictures, telling him how beautiful she thought they were and asking whether he knew anything about them. He sat her on his lap again on the cement steps and examined the brochure.

"Well, this is from what looks like a travel agency, which is a place that helps people go to different places around the world. I didn't even know they had these anymore. Look, it's called Compass Rose! These places look awesome, don't they?"

"Places like England?" Marie interjected, thinking of Grandad.

He smiled. "Yes, exactly. Only there's a lot of different countries all over the world. See this one?" he asked, pointing toward the shot of the beach. "These are islands in the Caribbean. It's a whole bunch of islands all surrounded by water where you sit in the sun all day and go swimming in the water."

Her eyes were wide, listening, so Shaun went on.

"The water is so clean, you can see everything through it. And you can look through goggles underwater and see the sand shifting with the waves, like wind is blowing them. The fish are all bright colors. Blue, orange with thick white stripes, neon green, light red, dark red, even purple."

"Purple?" Marie said, disbelieving. "That's my favorite."

"I know it! And the sand ..." he went on. "The sand is speckled with pink. You can scoop up a handful and pick out the bright pink, just like your shirt," he said, pulling on her rose-colored top. He smiled at her open mouth and continued, "Some islands are super crowded, but some are quiet, and you drive around in big jeeps on dirt roads, bouncing all over the place, because nothing is paved. It's the perfect temperature outside, so you can ride with the top down and the wind blowing in your hair." He lifted up Marie's hair as though that would make her understand. "You can dive down to the ocean floor and pick up huge shells that look like they have a rainbow living inside them."

Her blue eyes were large, filled with the images he was describing.

"And there's even caves around there. With bats and deep caverns that go underground for hours, with only a rope to hold onto so you don't get lost inside. It's all dark and dusky down there, and people have written things on the walls from years and years ago. And when you climb back out of the dark, you're looking at a beach, a beautiful ocean, and bright blue sky, and you would never guess that there's a whole other world down below the ground."

"That sounds amazing," Marie breathed.

When Marie went to bed, her mom was still in the bathroom. Shaun bent down to tuck Marie in. "Sweet dreams, darling," he whispered, climbing into the bed above her.

She closed her eyes, and visions of warm, sunny beaches danced into her head as she drifted to sleep …

—

It was dark, and all she could sense was a rough rope between her hands. The air was musty, like she was in a damp attic with little circulation. It was quiet except for an occasional pitter-patter. Marie wondered what it could be until she remembered her dad's story … bats. She wondered if they were watching her work her way through the dark cave. She closed her eyes and tried to be brave, silently telling the bats to stay put. She saw a light ahead and sped up, holding firmly to the rope lest she let go and find herself swallowed by the cave. The light soon was enough to see her surroundings.

Despite never liking the dark, she stopped to look around. She stood toward the bottom of an open area in the cave that continually sloped upward to the opening, where she could just barely see a patch of blue sky peering into the cave. The walls around her were dark brown. Some parts were lumpy and smooth. Some were sharp and jagged, little bits of the brown rock chipped off, leaving tiny ledges and lines. She thought for a moment that the cave was one huge hand with lines etched across its palm, reaching out to grab her. Marie scurried quickly into the opening, feeling that if she stayed any longer, the cave would keep her forever.

She found herself crawling out of the cave onto earth that seemed to be made of dirt, sand, and tall grass, with the heat of the sun blazing from above. The ground was warm to the touch, and she looked up, squinting against the bright glare, so different from the cool atmosphere of the cave. She gasped as she saw a little dirt path through the grass leading to a wide, white beach, just like the one in her brochure. She was frozen in a crawling position facing the beach, simply staring at her surroundings. A salty breeze lifted her hair, urging her to get up and walk toward the water. Soon her feet felt a different texture than the packed-down path, and the sand began to give way under her weight. She looked back at her footprints and saw them engraved where she had just stepped. Concrete had never done that! She continued to stare backward as she walked, amazed at the footsteps following her.

She was startled when she felt water tapping her toes. She whipped around and took in the scene, gasping in amazement. The water at her feet was the cleanest she had ever seen. Her parents had taken her once to a beach on the shore, but the water there had been dark and murky. Here, she could see her feet and ankles, looking strangely detached from the rest of her body standing in the shallow water. Small waves lapped gently at her legs and slid lazily onto the shore, then changed their mind and retreated back to the waters from which they emerged.

Marie remembered suddenly what her dad had said about the sand and scooped up a handful eagerly. As she brought it closer to her face, she could already see the pink specks of sand mixed with the white. Giggling in delight, she threw the sand up in the air, like confetti on New Year's, and spun around and around, kicking up water and poofs of sand that swirled around her feet in a chaotic frenzy.

"I'm in the prettiest ocean!" she shouted to the crystal-blue waters. They answered with the same gentle rhythm of the waves, not matching her excitement.

She had on a pink bathing suit with black polka dots, just like the one she had seen in the store, and her mother had said was too expensive. She noticed she had goggles on her head, and a snorkel attached. She remembered using it in the city pool the summer before, and she quickly splashed to deeper water to test it out. Something about the water made her feel as though she was born knowing how to swim, and how to peer at this underwater world. Her breathing sounded loud, like Darth Vader's, as she opened her eyes to look at what her father had described.

There was coral everywhere. It was blue, red, and purple, little kingdoms of what looked like huge sponges stretched across the floor. From above the water, they looked like mere shadows, but here, she was looking at the most detailed and amazing world she had ever seen. Fish of all shapes and sizes flipped to and fro, swimming through waving bits of seaweed, under mini tunnels. Some zoomed through the water on a mission, and some moseyed along as though they had not a care in the world.

One in particular was bright blue, probably no bigger than her hand, with black and yellow stripes down her side. It seemed to be smiling at Marie, so the delighted child followed it across the water. It curved in large shapes through the water, and Marie smiled as she tried to imitate the fish's movements. It brought her to an even bigger coral reef, where some logs with barnacles growing on them lay crisscrossed. Marie gasped at what she saw laying on the log.

It was a single rose, pink as the coral, beautiful and in full bloom. Marie immediately reached out her hand to grab it, and as her fingers closed around the stem, one of the logs let out a crack that sounded muffled underwater.

Its bark split, and barnacles hung off the sides, trying desperately to cling to their home. The log was hollow on the inside, and something glinted. Marie pulled back initially, but inched closer slowly, holding her breath to swim downward to see what was in the hollowed-out log. She reached in and felt her fingers close around a solid gold coin. Marie ogled at the shiny object, and right when she brought it closer to her face, everything vanished.

—

She lay on her bed and heard her father's rhythmic breathing. She was no longer in an ocean; the blankets of the trundle bed seemed very solid, and she quickly tried to remember every detail of her beautiful dream before it slipped away from the city night and back to the island where it belonged. She grinned at the thought of the sand, which had felt so real in her hands, and wondered as she drifted back to slumber about that rose she had held underwater and the gold piece she had found in the log.

Chapter 4

Shaun came home from a job that ran late, which was happening more often. While his schedule centering around Marie's needs as a baby had kept him from anything consistent then, he had recently taken a project manager position now that she was in school. Marie mostly didn't mind her mom those hours after school, waiting for him to get home; Olivia softened a bit when it was just the two of them. Marie tried to please her mother by doing her homework quietly or scooting outside to play in their small yard with a neighbor. Sometimes her mom washed dishes, sometimes she flipped through shiny magazines, and sometimes she just lay on the bed, smoking a cigarette. On the best days, she pulled out the crayons with Marie at the kitchen table and colored in Sesame Street coloring books. But every day around 4:30, they would always share two Oreos, playing the twist game and dipping them in a glass of milk. Olivia would have Marie snuggle up beside her on the old couch, a blanket covering both of them while they watched *I Love Lucy* together.

"Why does Oscar live in a trashcan, Mom?" Marie asked one day, filling in green carefully between Oscar the Grouch's lines.

Olivia, who was absentmindedly filling in Bert, looked over. "A trashcan? I don't know, seems weird to me," she answered.

Marie agreed, nodding and continuing to color. "I like our house. I'm glad you and Daddy found it."

Olivia's lips turned upward in a rare half-smile. "I'm glad, baby. I like it too."

Her mind swept up in the rhythm of coloring, concentrating hard, Marie answered, "Well sometimes you're grouchy like Oscar."

Never one to sugarcoat, Olivia didn't deny it, shrugging candidly. "Sometimes I'm a little tired and cranky. My job can be hard. Or I get a little bored."

Pointing at Olivia's near-finished picture of a purple Bert and Ernie, Marie looked at her mom and grimaced honestly. "Mom," she whispered, "you colored them wrong."

True to Shaun's demand, Olivia no longer drank in the afternoons. But the clearer her mind was in the day, the more Olivia wanted a break from the mundane. She was tired of feeling tired. Tired of feeling frumpy. Tired of the cool ashes that remained of the spark between her and Shaun. Tired of feeling worn down. She wanted something. Something to make her feel in control again. Something different.

**

"Where's Mommy?" Shaun asked, bending down to kiss Marie on the forehead as she stirred sleepily.

"Bathroom," answered Marie.

"How was school?" Shaun whispered, knowing he shouldn't keep Marie up but missing their usual bedtime routine, which grounded him.

She looked up at him, smiling. "I was the letter leader today."

"Of course you were," said Shaun. "What about our roses? Did you water them today?"

Her face lit up, and she nodded eagerly. "Yes! They're growing!" she said wondrously.

"My green-thumb girl," he whispered, pulling the blankets up around her chin, tucking her rabbit beside her. "I'll tell you another story about a place in the brochure in a minute, okay?"

Shaun heard the bathroom door close and stepped out to see Olivia. She met his eyes, which widened in surprise, then narrowed. As they did, she strode by, pushing the front door open and stepped outside. Shaun quietly followed in suit, closing the door firmly behind him. He stood on the sidewalk and looked Olivia up and down. She could see his jaw muscle working under his growing rusty beard.

She was dressed in black spiked sandals, with heels three inches off the ground. They extenuated the curve of her calf, the straps of her heels wrapped halfway up her ankle. Shaun briefly recalled his own hands following the lines of those straps, higher and higher up her leg. From the heels to where the slick black skirt began was *a lot* of leg; the skirt hugged the tops of her thighs and around her curvy hips. A simple silk top hung loosely from her shoulders, and he knew she wore nothing underneath it. Her hair fell straight and stylish, and she no longer looked tired; her makeup perfectly outlined the bold features of her face. His eyes met hers, and they held their locked gaze for several seconds. Her black eyes dared him to object. His blue ones dared her to explain.

"Well," he started.

Her glossy red lips turned slightly upward, the color making him think for a moment of the roses growing in the backyard.

"I'm going out," she said simply.

"Oh?" Shaun raised his eyebrows. "This isn't a grocery store run?"

"Don't be an ass," Olivia quipped back, eyes narrowing further.

He chuckled, the sound not reaching his eyes. "I don't think I'm the ass in this situation, honey."

"I'm not your wife, *darling.*"

"But you're a mother, Olivia." His tone matched hers— equally serious, equally heated.

"I didn't want to be."

Shaun looked back quickly, afraid Marie would be right behind him, hearing those words. The door was still closed tightly behind him. He took a deep breath to quell his anger. Count to ten, right? "Look, our agreement may not have been the best for us, but it was best for Marie." He opened his eyes and looked straight at her. "I mean, we aren't married, but we're something, Olivia. What are you trying to do tonight?"

"Does it matter?"

"It just doesn't feel right," Shaun answered. "Going wherever you're going. It would matter to me. Being unfaithful," he said slowly, his eyes taking in her outfit.

"Unfaithful, Shaun? Like you're one to talk," Olivia shot back, looking expectantly at him. "What about her?"

"Her who?" Shaun said, his eyebrows drawing in, taken off guard. "There's been no one, Olivia."

She sighed again. "The name you say in your sleep is not mine, Shaun." She paused, watching his face freeze. Her voice continued, softer. "The times we're … together … I know you're not thinking of me. We're both unfaithful, Shaun. Marie's got a place in your heart; I've got no doubt about that. And that's good, 'cause I'm a shitty mother, and she needs somebody." Olivia shifted in her heels. "But I've got no real place with you; maybe I almost did once, but I know you dream of another girl." She pulled a pack of cigarettes out of her purse, tapped them lightly on her palm, and put one in her mouth. "That's why I said no," she said through her lips, her face illuminated for an instant from the lighter's flame at the tip of the cigarette.

26

"Why you said no?" This was the only statement Shaun's mind wrapped around quickly enough to respond to.

She pulled the now burning cigarette out, holding it between her fingers and blowing the smoke out of her red lips. The smoke curled around her face in a fog, and she waved it away. "When you asked me to marry you six years ago."

His mouth was slightly open as he stared at her, motionless. She leaned forward, kissed his cheek slowly, and turned to walk to the bus stop, her heels clicking on the sidewalk. Shaun stood in front of the house, a lone silhouette against the warming spring air.

He closed the door quietly behind him, still slightly lost in the thoughts Olivia had sent swirling around his head. He looked over to find Marie out of bed, watching him, her eyebrows drawn together and frowning with concern.

"Where's Mommy going?" she asked, her voice light and anxious.

Shaun ran his fingers through his hair to bring himself back into reality and plopped down next to Marie. "She's going to a party."

"Without you?"

"Yeah … I didn't really want to anyway. Just a bunch of silly adults who are all dressed up." He made a face at her to convey that he wasn't impressed with this social group and would much rather spend his Friday night at home with her.

"Daddy, you can go if you want to be with Mommy," Marie said quietly. "She looks fancier than normal."

"Are you crazy? And miss our date with our fancy travel brochure?" He laughed and pulled her onto his lap. "I don't think so, missy. Go get those pictures and pick which one you want a story about. And then it's back to bed for you."

Marie made a beeline to the bedroom and zoomed back with the brochure in hand. She sat down on Shaun's lap again, closed her eyes, and let her finger fall to one of the pictures. They both bent down to peer at which one it was. "Ahhh …" said Shaun, smiling at last. "Scotland." "Scotland …" Marie breathed, as though she already knew everything about it. "What's it like, Daddy?" He shifted, stretching out his long legs and crossing them, leaning back against the couch and folding his hands behind his head, a perfect storyteller's stance.

"Scotland is majestic," he said.

"What does 'majestic' mean?" Marie asked, waiting with bright eyes.

"It means it is magical and powerful, like a queen. There are mountains so huge there that when you stand on them, you feel like a speck of dirt resting on their side. There aren't any trees on these mountains, so you know they aren't trying to hide anything from you. They don't have to. They are so beautiful, so green, so enormous, rolling through the deep valleys of Scotland, that people just stop and stare at them. They call them the Highlands."

"Are they alive?" Marie cut in, trying to imagine herself on the side of one of these mountains.

"Of course they're alive!" said Shaun. "They are strong and brave. They have the same stuff as their people, you know."

Marie shook her head.

"Ah, their hearts beat with a fierce love for Scotland. The Scots are so proud to live in such a fine country with such fine people. So many times, especially in the olden days, other countries came in and tried to take over their land. But the people loved Scotland so much that they would fight to keep it, to keep their families and their lands and their mountains safe, in the hands of the people who truly loved it. And the mountains came alive with that love and seemed to swell under the Earth, rising tall to protect the people who loved them so much."

"Wooow," breathed Marie, trying to fathom this foreign land, so different from the pink beaches he had described earlier. "Is it warm there?" she asked, remembering her dream of the blazing sun on the beach.

Shaun laughed. "Not exactly. The reason the Highlands are so green is because it rains all the time. And it's not yucky and polluted. It's clean, and the land soaks it up like a sponge and holds it. Do you know what else?"

"No," said Marie, completely mesmerized.

"There are lakes on top of some of the mountains. Not just streams that spill down the sides of them, but huge lakes that sit right on top of the mountain, like a mirror for the sky."

Marie's small mouth dropped open. "Real lakes?"

"Rrrrrreal lakes!" Shaun responded, rolling his r's in his best Scottish accent. "You know what else?"

"What? What?"

"The men wear skirts."

Marie's hand flew to her mouth and a giggle escaped. "The *boys* wear *skirts*? Don't they feel silly?"

"Not at all," Shaun said, completely serious. "They all do it. They probably think we're weird for wearing pants."

"Dad, how do you know so much about these places? Did you go to them?"

Shaun waved his hand in the air. "Only a few. But I had big plans to go see the whole world right after college." He sighed almost happily. "We were going to go everywhere we could, with nothing but a backpack."

"Why didn't you go?"

A shadow crossed Shaun's face. He seemed to shake it off, and then scooped up Marie. "I was waiting for you! We'll go see all of these places when you're older, on daddy-daughter adventures together!"

"Scotland first!" cried Marie.

"Scotland it is."

Marie giggled again as Shaun brought her to the bedroom. "It's past your bedtime now, Marie. Brush your teeth, and let's climb in bed!"

—

Marie felt the burning in her small thigh as she climbed uphill. She stepped over rocks, some smaller than the nickels in her piggy bank, others larger than a basketball. Some were even as big as her desk at school. The air was cool, damp, and fresh. Looking around, she gasped. Her father was right.

They were majestic.

Marie turned around to face every different direction; she could hear herself breathing in the crisp Highlands air. It was not dirty like the city, not salty like the Bahamas. Just clean.

The mountains were indeed enormous, vast, an earthly green, rolling over the land to stand towering over her. She had the feeling they were protecting her with the magic Shaun had told her about, and she could feel the love of the land pulsing through her. It had just rained, and Marie could feel the enormity of the sky and its possibilities under her feet. Her jaw dropped again as she gazed at a stream falling gracefully down the surface of the tall mountain, like a sliding waterfall. No trees blocked her vision; the Highlands opened their soul for her to see every inch.

Even her insides felt the magic here. Feeling as though her heart was growing, Marie climbed on again. She wanted to reach the top. Step after step, she knew her muscles were growing stronger. Her sneakers were dirty and getting worn down, but she didn't mind.

Finally, she reached the top, and there it was. A lake stretched out on top of a mountain.

"Holy moly," she whispered to the Highlands.

The surface was completely peaceful and calm, knowing the surrounding gatekeepers would keep its secret safe. She was at a dizzying height and felt almost light-headed; she wondered, if she just stood on her tip-toes, would her fingers brush the sky?

She stared at the glasslike reflection that the lake painted, a watercolor of blurry mountains and a vast sky, dark greens and grays blending together with mercury silver dancing through each image. She suddenly noticed another reflection near her.

It was a grown man, clad in a crimson kilt and tartan. His hair was as long as hers, but it was a lighter brown, thick and wavy across his shoulders, a friendly beard covering his chin and cheeks. He wore a loose white shirt that made the plaid pattern stand out even more boldly, a large piece of fabric thrown over his shoulder. The kilt surprisingly did not look foolish; in fact, he looked as majestic as the mountains themselves. His eyes were smiling and kind. In his hand was a single rose.

"Do you grow roses, too?" she asked, her hands respectfully clasped behind her back.

The Highlander squatted down to her level and motioned her forward with a jerk of his head, his face good-natured and caring. He held out the beautiful rose. "Bring this to yer faither."

"To Daddy?"

He nodded once, his eyes looking right into hers.

She took it, her gaze not moving from his. Their faces were close together. One soft, with chubby cheeks, long lashes, and child-like roundness; the other, strong with high cheekbones, weathered, and wise. She brought her nose to the rose's soft petals, breathing in the gentle beauty.

—

When she opened her eyes again, she was back by her father's side, listening to the quiet sounds of the house at night. The green of the mountains had faded around her, leaving only thin white walls and the city around them, cars running and sirens wailing in the distance. But she could still smell the sweet rose as she took a deep breath. She remembered the Highlander and his kind eyes.

Bring this to your father.

Chapter 5

"I … I don't understand," said Annie, her eyes scanning the pair who stood in front of her. "My parents found out two years after I left. You died in a car accident. I saw the article in the newspaper, the picture of the wreck, everything. I wrote a letter to your parents. I was so … upset. I got a letter back saying Jerry had passed away. It said your family had moved. I thought … I thought you were both gone."

"You're Annie," whispered Marie from Shaun's side. It was not a question; she was not surprised. Only a hint of curiosity and hope touched her voice.

Shaun's face snapped to Marie's, his jaw open and heart pace quickening. "Sweetie, how do you know her?" Marie did not answer, and a shy dimple peeked through one cheek at the trace of a smile on her face.

"Oh my gosh …" murmured the woman to herself. She stared at Marie's familiar smile. "She's your daughter." She looked up to Shaun. "You have a little girl." Her brilliant green eyes welled with tears, her breath catching in her chest, knowing those blue eyes and dimples on the child.

Shaun was still, moments unfolding that he hadn't ever imagined would happen. He swallowed, and in a choked voice said, "Annie, this is my daughter, Marie Charlotte Murray."

"Marie Charlotte ..." she whispered, the corners of her mouth turning upward for a moment. "Marie, honey, how do you know who I am?"

Marie looked up at the two adults. "I already told you. I followed the roses."

Chapter 6

Marie continued to dream of the places her father told her about each night. A routine began to form through their small house. Shaun walked Marie to the school bus stop every morning as usual before going to work until dinner time. Marie came home from school around three o'clock. Some days, Olivia was at the stop to pick her up, magazine in hand; other days, Marie ran home by herself. Some days, she brought a friend, and they played in the garden, picking beetles off the roses, checking for black spots, or getting lost in the world of six-year-old imagination. When Marie was alone, she spoke to the roses, encouraging them to grow, or sang Beyoncé, which she was still sure was the best method.

She began to notice roses everywhere—in her dreams, in real life. Even the travel brochure was from a company called "Compass Rose" and had a large sketch of the flower on the front. She decided the roses were from Grandad, like Shaun had said, and that he was checking in on her, letting her know he was there with her even though they'd never met.

Olivia cooked dinner some nights; on others, she claimed she was too tired, and Shaun would make macaroni and cheese and hot dogs. The two parents ignored each other for the most part. Marie dared not tell her father, but sometimes she found bottles hidden in Olivia's drawers, hearing them clank when Olivia put another in as Marie loyally did her homework on the kitchen table. The small kitchen was open to the living room, separated only by a counter, so when Marie played by the toy shelf by their couch and TV, she could see Olivia aimlessly opening cabinets, looking for something she never seemed to find. When Shaun arrived home, Olivia grabbed her purse and stalked out of the door in her pink outfit with barely a hello or goodbye to him. Shaun would plop down on their rug, and he and Marie would often compete in building contests with the small box of colorful Legos Santa had brought the year before.

Shaun's tales about the pictures in the Compass Rose brochure took both of them away from the stresses in the house. His stories always left Marie full of visions of beautiful places that visited her in her sleep; she looked forward to bed each night, knowing she would find a rose leading to some wonderful treasure.

One night, her dreams took her to the desert; Shaun said it was a sunbeam that had hit the Earth just right and burst into a thousand pieces that spread to form the sand. Marie believed him as she crossed the sprawling, barren, and bright piece of sun on Earth. She found the rose growing on a ridge, and on the other side lay an oasis: lush, cool, and full of life.

Another night she traveled to Ghana, where she danced under the night sky to the sound of a beating drum and a chorus of strong, beautiful voices. A little boy, his skin beautifully black and his eyes deep chocolate pools, brought her a crimson rose that looked like it was minutes away from full bloom. He grinned at her and nodded his head up toward the sky; Marie gasped as she saw one of the millions of stars that pierced the sky grow brighter, twinkling and sparkling brilliantly. Marie knew it was looking right at her.

She went to castles in England, a plaza in Spain, volcanoes in Hawaii, and snow-covered mountains in Switzerland. She traveled to Vietnamese villages, jungles in South America, and sailed in the middle of a blue, blue ocean that stretched as far as the eye could see. And in every dream, she found a rose that led to a treasure. She wanted to tell her dad about the dreams, but they were so special that she knew she had to wait for the perfect moment.

One night, she pointed to the picture of a path curving through a forest wrapped in Autumn's colors of red, orange, and yellow.

"Where's this, Daddy?"

He was staring at the description written below, dropping that curtain of calm over his face that hid any emotion. The only sign of his thoughts was his jaw working under his short, rusty beard.

She peered closely at the words. "Mmmm ... Maaa ..."

"Maple Falls," Shaun said, his voice sounding far away. "Maple Falls, North Carolina."

"Maple Falls," Marie repeated. "Where's that?"

"It's where I grew up," he answered, surprising himself with how simply he was speaking about his old home.

"You lived here?" Marie goggled, looking back at the picture.

He nodded. "Yes. For many, many years."

The questions spilled out from Marie. "What did your house look like? Did Grandad live there too? Where was your mommy? Did you have brothers and sisters?"

"Slow down, little hoss!" Shaun laughed in spite of the tightness in his chest. "Let's start with one question at a time. Let's see ... We lived in a neighborhood where kids were always riding their bikes and climbing trees. Our house had forest-green shutters and two huge magnolia trees in

37

front that my brothers, my sister, and I climbed all the time. The backyard was Grandad's garden."

Marie prodded, "You had brothers *and* a sister?"

Shaun nodded, afraid to wonder what they were doing now, afraid to open that door. His tone carefully masked the depth of emotion he felt as he allowed himself to answer her basic question. "Two brothers and a sister. And our mom was always cooking; she was so full of bubbly energy." He was surprised that the tightness eased the more he talked, the more he let himself remember.

Marie stared up at him, questions piling up in her mind, wanting to know more. She couldn't imagine having three siblings. Not being able to pick one question out of so many, she asked, "Why did you leave?"

"Some things happened," Shaun said, his voice suddenly tight again and his jaw stiff. "I, well ... I just had to go."

"Are they still there?" dug Marie in her six-year-old way. "What happened?"

"Oh ..." Shaun waved his hand lightly, although his chest felt suddenly very heavy. "I needed some thinking time, I guess."

"What about your family? What happened to your family?"

"I just told them I had to go; I think they understood."

"Don't they want you to come back?"

Shaun made a noncommittal noise in his throat. "That's not really a story for right now," he said, standing up and scooping up his daughter to go put on pajamas.

"I don't get it." Marie scowled at him, wanting to know the rest of the story.

"It means time for little girls to be in bed. Go brush your teeth, Marie."

—

Marie wandered through the path in the woods from the brochure, except it was summer, not autumn. The trees were green and full, alive in color. The trees leaned over the trail to make a ceiling of a thousand leaves and branches, allowing only bits of sunlight to filter through them. If she could have built a cathedral, she would have painted the ceiling like the trees that enveloped her, giving her a feeling of peace and closeness to the forest. The tunnel of trees she walked through eventually led her to an opening where she could see fields sprawled in front of her, rolling gently over the land in a lazy summer spirit.

The grass was tall and uncut, tickling her hands as she brushed them walking by. Each blade of grass squeaked in delight whenever she ran her fingers tightly down the edge. She put a strand of wheat in her mouth, feeling like a farmer tasting its dry sweetness. She meandered down the slope, in no hurry, taking in the mild hills, looking back at the woods by the edge of the fields, enjoying the feel of the tall grass grazing her palms.

She stopped suddenly at a clearing at the bottom of the hill. Her father was sitting in a chair with a glass of lemonade, and behind him sprawled the biggest, most beautiful rose garden Marie had ever seen. There were dozens and dozens of bushes—hundreds of pink, yellow, red, and white roses dancing in front of her, their colors standing out against the dark green of their leaves. Some were huge, blooming wide and overflowing with petals. Others were still wrapped tightly, wanting to keep their secret for a little while longer. Marie could barely stop gazing at the wealth of roses.

Her gaze traveled back to her father, who looked happier than she had ever seen him, glowing in the sea of roses. His face did not look tired at all; it looked healthy and vibrant. He was laughing at something, and she followed his gaze to see what it was.

She was surprised to see two other people working side by side in the garden, laughing with Shaun. One was a tall woman with light brown skin, her curly black hair pulled into a ponytail and her vivid green eyes sparkling with amusement. She wore a floppy straw hat, but her face was dark and a bit pink from the sun, freckles sprinkled across her cheeks. Marie immediately liked her. She was holding a watering can, and judging from the large wet spot on her T-shirt that Shaun was pointing at, she had been watering herself more than the flowers.

Marie noticed the second person, a man chuckling by the woman's side. She knew in an instant who he was. He wore good black shoes and a fine white shirt neatly tucked into ironed gray trousers. His gray hair was parted to one side, and his eyes were kind and pleasant. He was trimming a bush with complete care, and she knew the garden was proudly his.

It was Grandad.

—

She woke suddenly. She shook her head, trying to get her bearings, struggling to remember the people in her dream and the beautiful garden. Olivia had come into the room and was trying to open her drawer quietly. She was watching Shaun with her glistening dark eyes, making sure he was still asleep as she pulled out a box from the very back of the drawer. Marie did not move a muscle, curious as to what her mother was doing.

Olivia slipped a bill from her pocket into the box, the money folded into a small, neat square. She was about to close the box when she paused and bit her lip, lifting an old, worn piece of paper from the box. Olivia looked at it for a moment and slowly unfolded it. The creases had been there for ages, and the paper looked like it could have never been fresh or crisp. Marie could see her mother's eyes darting back and forth, reading the scrolling words on the other side, still biting her lip in deliberation.

She looked at Shaun for a moment with her brows drawn in in concern, and then they lowered further in anger, as though she was having an inner conversation no one else could hear. She closed her eyes tightly and put the piece of paper back into the box, setting it in the drawer, which she closed softly. She had emptied out the clanking bottles, so that only scattered clothes hid the wooden box at the back of the drawer.

Marie let her eyelids drop, hoping when she fell asleep she would drift away, back to the beautiful rose garden where her grandad was working so carefully to keep them thriving and where Shaun sipped lemonade carelessly in a lawn chair, laughing with the woman in the straw hat and freckles.

Chapter 7

Shaun had still not gotten his bearings. He bent down to his daughter, struggling to stay calm.

"You followed the roses?" he asked, having no idea what she meant.

"The roses always lead to something special," Marie said, matter-of-fact. "I have dreams about the places you tell me about, and every time I find a rose, it brings me to a treasure." She paused for a moment. Her fingers reached into her pocket and pulled out a folded piece of paper. She heard Annie take in her breath quickly, and Shaun looked back and forth from Marie, to the paper, to Annie.

"Oh God …" breathed Annie, sounding as though something was stuck in her chest. She grabbed at the top of her shirt, holding her heart.

Marie held the paper out to Shaun. "Mommy kept this in a box in her drawer," she said apologetically, knowing she shouldn't have snooped. "I know it says A-N-N-I-E at the bottom. Like the movie. Annie. And I could read the word 'rose,' so I thought maybe it was a sign, like Grandad sends you."

"Oh my god …" echoed Shaun, unfolding it and seeing the words.

Dear Jerry,

From the day I first met you in the garden shop, you, Charlotte, and your family opened your arms to me. You gave me something hopeful to hold on to. You gave me a true sense of family. I knew I could turn to you when things got chaotic and stressful, and you would tell me to take a deep breath and calm me down. Even when the worst happened with my parents and Shaun, you were kind and constant. I will never forget your thoughtfulness to me.

I was almost your daughter in-law, and as so, I am finally writing to express my sorrow for Shaun. Sorrow cannot begin to describe it, this shock, this unbearable grief that I have no idea what to do with. I am so sorry that I've been gone and that I did not find out about his death until now. You must miss him terribly.

I cannot explain how much I regret not standing up to my parents. I wish I could have seen that before it was too late. I am so sorry, Jerry, for the way I have acted, for my lack of courage.

I want to come back to Maple Falls. Please write back to this address. I want to be a part of your family's life again.

Shaun was a gift. I am honored to have been loved by him, and I am heartbroken that I let it go.

I have never forgotten our days in the rose garden with you and your family. Please let Charlotte and the others know how sorry I am. You all are in my thoughts.

With love as always,
Annie

Shaun burst into the house with Marie at his heels.

"Olivia! Olivia!" he called, his voice deep and stocked with emotion.

She wandered out from the bedroom. "What?"

"You know about Annie?"

Olivia's nonchalant mood vanished instantly at Annie's name spoken out loud, a name she had heard only softly in the dark hours of the night from Shaun's sleeping mind and seen only scrawled at the bottom of the hidden letter. Hearing him say it aloud and purposefully was so unexpected, and it shocked her out of her usual casual indifference.

"Yeah," she said tensely.

"Yeah, anything you forgot to mention over the last six years?"

"Like what?"

"Like what? You tell me." His tone was fierce and unrelenting, barely containing the rage he so obviously felt. Olivia had never seen such a fire in his eyes. She should have known this day would come.

"All right," she said, cursing to herself. "Let's talk."

They stepped into the bedroom that seemed too small to hold the charged air vibrating throughout the house.

Marie stared out of the window, almost hoping to see Annie walking down the sidewalk to their house. She knew something was changing; Shaun had told Annie he would not lose her again.

PART II

"Oh crap!"

Packets of seeds, a watering can, and two seedlings of small green plants flew out of her arms and into the aisle. The can clamored to the floor loudly; a couple packets burst open, and dirt from the seedlings sprawled across the way. "I'm sorry, sir; I totally did not see you coming!"

The older gentleman steadied himself, then the young woman who had slammed into him. "That's quite all right; quite all right. You must have been in a hurry. I'm sorry for having slowed you down," he said, chuckling and bending down to help her gather her strewn items. She heard a hint of British in his accent that caught her attention and made her frantic reactions slow down.

"Oh, no, it's really fine," she said as she helped him brush the dirt into a pile. "I was just in my own little world going around the corner. Are you all right? I bumped into you pretty hard."

He laughed gently. "Don't let this gray hair fool you; I'm sturdier than I look." He held out a strong hand. "My name is Jerry Murray; pleased to meet you."

She shook his hand and smiled. "Annie Johnson. it's nice to meet you too."

"Planning a garden?" he asked, nodding at the items she was holding. His tone was kind and straightforward, much like his appearance. He wore gray slacks, a white button-up shirt with a plain white handkerchief tucked neatly into the breast pocket, and well-kept black shoes. Both his eyes and smile were warm and oddly calming for her.

"I'm not sure yet." Her freckled nose wrinkled in thought, and she sighed audibly. "I've been living off campus from the college for a little while in a house my best friend and I rent, and we want to make it homier, even though we only have a few months left." She shrugged at him. "I figured maybe a garden might work. I've never tried one though. I'm not sure how green my thumb will be."

Jerry nodded. "Well I myself am a rose-grower. I've been gardening for a long time, so I could give you some tips if you'd like."

"Roses!" Annie's face lit up. "Can I buy those here?"

"Last one right here," he said, holding out the potted bush he had tucked under his arm, offering it to her.

"Oh no, you were going to buy that. I don't know how to take care of them anyway."

He shook his head. "Go ahead, take it. I have dozens of bushes at home, and a few waiting to be planted as well. I used to get my children to help me tend to them, but now that they're growing up, my labor force is steadily decreasing. I really don't need another bush to look after. You take it; I'll help you care for it if you'd like."

Annie smiled somewhat shyly. "Well thank you very much; that's very kind of you." She took the bush from him and sat back on her heels for more of a conversational pose. "You said you have children?"

"Four of them," he answered with no small hint of pride in his voice. They brushed the dirt into little piles at their feet while they talked. "Three boys and a girl. The oldest, Shaun, is about your age, I believe." He squinted, taking in her appearance. "Twenty-three this month."

"I'll be twenty-two this fall." Then she whistled. "Well, four kids. Man ..."

"Do you have brothers and sisters?"

"Nope. Just me. I'm an only." Annie wrinkled her nose again, somewhat regretfully. "Wouldn't mind some brothers and sisters sometimes. Being the only kid can get lonely."

"I'm sure it can," Jerry sympathized, thinking of his own chaotic household and what it would be like with only one child. Then again, imagining the quiet reverie that could follow, he smiled. "I suppose each side has its advantages."

"I suppose so," said Annie, not entirely convinced. She caught sight of a clock on the garden shop's wall. "Shoot! I have to get to class in fifteen minutes! My professor is going to kill me if I'm late again." She glanced frantically at the only slightly cleaner mess on the floor.

"Don't worry about that. I'm a regular here. I'll help Midge clean up." He guided her toward the door. "How about I'll have that rose bush at my house, and you can come by Saturday and get it, and I'll give you some pointers. Do you know Priscilla Lane?"

The town was the size of a thimble; it took her two seconds to conjure the street's location.

"We are toward the end of that," Jerry responded to her nod. "Number 659. You're welcome anytime."

"Six-fifty-nine. Got it. Well, thank you so much, Jerry. It was wonderful to meet you." Annie pulled her keys out of her purse and pushed the door open, the bell above it ringing cheerfully as she walked quickly to her car, all supplies forgotten. Jerry laughed and gathered them up to deliver that weekend. He turned to find Midge smiling at him.

"Make a new friend, Jer?" she asked, rearranging pots toward the back. She and Jerry had been friends for years as he frequented the little garden shop; they used to sit outside during her breaks while Jerry read up on the latest gardening tips from her magazines. They talked about their children and yards and plants, and she enjoyed watching him interact with her customers, helping them if she was busy.

"Well," he said, pulling up a chair to visit. "Either a new rose bush or a new friend; either one will do."

**

Annie rang the doorbell somewhat nervously. "Six-five-nine," she repeated, looking at the iron numbers hung on the brick wall of the house. "This is the place."

"You're going *where?*" her best friend, Zoe, had asked skeptically earlier that morning when Annie explained her errand.

"It's fine, Zo; he was like a sweet grandpa."

"Mmmmhmmm. He wasn't a predator grandpa, was he?" Zoe said with a zing in her voice, as always. "Did you look him up or anything?"

Annie laughed and shook her head. "If I'm not back by tonight, you can call up the police and tell them your theories, but I think it's just a nice old man who could tell I don't know a thing about gardens. It's a small town here; people are just nice for no reason."

Zoe tipped her head to the side. "Well, he's not wrong about you not knowing anything about a garden. I don't know why you want to plant stuff now anyway. I mean, we'll both be graduating this year. You don't really want to put roots down here. Metaphorically, I mean," she interjected before Annie could make a lame pun as she loved to do.

With a shrug of her shoulders, Annie leaned up against their kitchen counter. "I don't know. I sure don't want to move back near my folks. Imagine that torture."

Zoe grimaced and shook her head. "No thanks, boo. Your mama scares the crap out of me when she visits. She's always telling me my goals aren't good enough."

Annie said, "See? I could stay here. Write for the paper. Teach in a school. Really blow their plans for me out of the water."

Leaning across the table, wiggling her eyebrows, Zoe suggested, "Or travel the world like you always talk about. Backpack across Europe. Surf in Costa Rica! Hike a glacier!"

"I don't even know how to surf," Annie dismissed, though a tiny voice inside her wanted to yell "YES," something she rarely let herself say. Impulsive decisions had been stamped out of her mode of operation since day one.

"Don't know how to surf? So learn," Zoe replied, giving Annie a pointed look, grabbing an apple and waving as she disappeared into the hallway to her room.

Just a few hours later, Annie leaned over the porch at her new friend's house, struggling to see if there was any movement inside. Was eleven o'clock too early? Lunchtime? Maybe she shouldn't have come. Zoe could be right; people were crazy these days.

At least she was able to cancel lunch with her mother, who liked to make the drive some weekends to ensure Annie was staying on top of things, living up to her impossible expectations. Denise Johnson was everything Annie was not: always sharply dressed, always on time, always with the best purse, fashion, car, or whatever it was she thought people cared about. She was the type who criticized food in restaurants and glanced warily at people she didn't approve of, but she always had a false laugh ready if the situation called for charm. Fake. Annie found herself cringing automatically as her thoughts drifted to her mother.

Shaking her head to clear her mind, Annie leaned forward once more to knock. She was just about to rap lightly when she heard noises from behind the house. She walked curiously along the sidewalk that wound past the side of the house, the garage on one side of her and huge holly bushes on the other. She peered around the corner of the house to see a tall man spraying a hose toward a potted plant but accidentally hitting a much smaller middle-aged woman, who darted behind a short half-wall of ivy that surrounded the little patio.

"Shaun! Put that hose down!" the lady yelped, ducking when he yelled "Whoops!" and squirted another shoot of water in her direction. "You will be grounded, young man!"

"Ma, I'm twenty-three! I don't think you can ground me anymore!" Shaun hollered back.

"You're barely twenty-three yet, Shaun Joseph Murray! And I am your mother! I have grounding rights until you're fifty!"

Shaun looked over toward Jerry, who was laughing. "Better listen to her, Shaun. I've been dealing with that woman for more than twenty-five years, and she's not kidding."

As he turned to the rose bushes behind him, Annie stared, amazed at the spread of the rose garden. She had never seen so many bushes together. Most of the buds were still camping out in protective green leaves, but she could just barely start to see small colors beginning to poke their heads out to see if warm weather was around for good. She could barely start to imagine what it must look like in the summer. There must have been over fifty bushes lining the wooden fence around the yard.

"Are you going to be around for the afternoon, Shaun?" his mother asked, coming out of her hiding place behind the wall as he wound up the hose.

"Nah, I think Billy and I are going to go play some football with some of the boys, and then I'll head back to my townhouse. I've got a couple jobs to work on tomorrow at the university—deadlines for the new building permit and stuff."

Annie was peering further around the corner to see the rest of the yard when Jerry spotted her. "Annie! Hello! You decided to stop by!"

"Um, yes, here I am for my first lesson," she said, smoothing her T-shirt and stepping forward as Jerry crossed the yard toward her. "I see I've got quite the collection to learn from." She nodded toward the wide expanse of rose bushes behind Jerry.

"Oh, a few, yes. Well, I'm so glad you are here." Jerry smiled, beckoning her further into the backyard. "Annie, this is my better half, Charlotte."

"Pleased to meet you," said Annie, holding out her hand.

"You're the young lady Jerry met at Midge's shop, hmm? It's lovely to meet you too, dear. Good to see Jerry wasn't making things up. Would you like anything to eat?"

"No, ma'am." Annie shook her head, tucking stray hairs behind her ears where they rarely liked to stay put.

"Anything to drink?" Charlotte asked, opening the screen door to step inside the back doorway to the house.

"No ma'am, I'm fine, thank you."

"I'll bring you out some sweet tea and this bread experiment I just tried out. It might be terrible, but it just might be delicious. You'll have to tell me." Before Annie could open her mouth in response, the door slammed behind the petite woman, and Annie was left in mid-breath.

Jerry chuckled and motioned her to a chair on the patio. "My guess is the latter. She doesn't take no for an answer, especially when it comes to food. Ran her own catering business for years while taking care of four wild children too. Here, you can have a seat if you'd like."

Shaun came back from around the other side of the house where he had disappeared to put away a hose, wiping the sweat off his ruddy brow. He glimpsed at her and nodded casually, then turned quickly back to her face, eyebrows raised.

Annie sat, glancing at Jerry for direction as Shaun failed to recover his surprise. She tried not to eye him too awkwardly.

"Ah, this is my eldest son, Shaun. He was just helping with the garden this morning, amazingly enough. Like I told you, the older they get, the harder it is to get them out here. Shaun, this is Annie; we met in Midge's shop. She wants to learn to grow roses."

Shaun blinked, realizing he was staring at Annie. He shook it off, grinned, and nodded toward her. "Hey there, nice to meet you. Sorry, I thought Dad met someone his age at the garden shop. You're a little younger than I expected."

"Well, yes, I suppose so."

Annie silently cursed herself for not even glancing in the mirror before she left. While Zoe—tall and thin—flaunted all the latest fashions, Annie always felt more self-conscious trying to look presentable. She often stuck to soft cotton T-shirts and athletic shorts in the summer, and big sweaters with jeans in the winter. Curves had been a part of her life since she was in middle school, and the thought of a thigh gap was laughable. But as obsessed as her mother was with the perfect body image, Annie leaned the opposite way, accepting her curves and celebrating comfort. Mostly people noticed her eyes anyway, bright green against her darker complexion, and her wide smile. It looked like Shaun was no exception.

"You're learning from the best," he said, a dirty hand gesturing toward Jerry, who was pruning a bush he'd been eyeing. "New to this whole rose thing, huh?"

"Yes, I'm afraid I don't know much about it at all." She gestured at the roses. "I take it you're pretty used to being out here?"

He laughed easily, a dimple appearing in each cheek. Built solidly with just a little softness to him, he stood several inches taller than Annie. He had a wide jaw covered in stubble, a sharp nose, and ruddy skin; it looked like he spent a good bit of time outdoors. "Well, not by choice. Dad was forever making us work with the roses when we were growing up. Or punishing us for messing them up."

"Oh?" Annie laughed.

"He made my brothers and me sleep outside one night when we were rough-housing and tackled each other into a white bush. He just put down three sleeping bags on the patio for the night, didn't have to say a word. So, you know, don't mess up today helping out," he added with a grin.

Annie laughed again, briefly mentally comparing his story to her own punishments growing up, which typically involved polishing silver or being banished to her room in silence. Punishments were lonely and tedious in the Johnson household. In fact, most of her childhood was lonely and tedious.

"Don't you go telling horror stories on me now," called Jerry. "She's only just come; we can't scare her off yet."

As if on cue, another boy came out of the house, probably around eighteen years old. He was wirier, wearing jeans with gaping holes in the knees and a white dirty T-shirt with a bandana around his head, his long dark hair pulled back into a ponytail.

"Hey, what's up, dude?" Shaun said, his voice retreating into a deeper tone.

"Nothing, man. You ready to play football?"

Shaun lifted one side of his face in hesitation and shrugged. "Eh, I don't know if I'm going today. I'll catch y'all tomorrow with it."

"Man, Shaun, come on ..."

Shaun shrugged again. "I have some paperwork to get done for that job next week."

"Whatever. You've never turned down a game for work; what's up?" He rolled his eyes and suddenly spotted Annie. "Oh," he said.

"Billy, this is Annie; she's learning to grow roses from Dad. Annie, this is my brother, Billy." Shaun gestured at the both of them during the introductions and shoved his hands in his old cargo shorts when he was through.

Billy nodded at Annie. "How's it going?"

"All right," she answered, still taking in the family around her. Despite her shyness, she found herself warming up surprisingly fast.

"Glad to hear it. All right, Shaun, I'm out then. Good luck with that paperwork and all," he said, grinning at the both of them. "Annie, enjoy those roses. See you guys."

As he walked away, tossing the football in the air to himself, Charlotte bustled out with a tray in hand. "I've got the sweet tea! Sorry it took so long! Tara called on the phone wanting to know if the boys could help move furniture tomorrow, and then Margaret called from across the street to check to see how Liza was feeling so I had to fill her in on that—she got mono a month ago," Charlotte explained to Annie, not missing a beat. "Half the class has it, sharing drinks and God knows what else. These high schoolers don't have a lick of sense. At any rate, that reminded me to call the doctor to see when Liza is cleared to be a normal, active human again. I tell ya, the fun never ends. Anyway, Annie, darling, eat up; don't let Shaun steal them all. Shaun, weren't you going to play football?"

"He's got, um, paperwork?" answered Annie, the corners of her mouth curling up.

Shaun turned a bit pinker, a dimple appearing again.

"Uh huh …" laughed Charlotte knowingly, handing Annie a napkin.

Jerry had gathered some supplies and lined them up in front of the rose garden. "Annie, when you're done with the food, come on over, and Shaun and I will show you the basics. How long can you stay today?"

"I'm free all day," she said, feeling a sense of relief and comfort she had seldom felt sitting around with her own parents. *I wonder if this is what family is supposed to be*, she thought to herself. *If this is what home is supposed to feel like.*

"Great," said Jerry. "I'll show you how to do the pruning once the plant is in the ground."

"You're actually going to let her prune the bushes?" Shaun asked, stopping halfway through biting his piece of bread. "Day one?" He looked back toward Annie. "He must trust you for some reason," he whispered.

Annie glanced at Jerry, who was laughing, shaking his head at Shaun. "She looks like she's got a calm way about her, unlike you and your wild siblings. You brood could weed, kill the beetles, check for black spot, water them, but you were always eager to be done; pruning takes patience."

Annie smiled at his reasoning, while Shaun looked at Jerry skeptically. She looked back at the garden and could practically see Jerry's patience and consistent care in the blooms. She could see how fragile they were and figured perhaps he was right; maybe she could do this.

She brushed the crumbs off her hand and hopped up to learn the art of pruning, leaving Shaun to finish and watch her go by, nearly bursting with curiosity about her.

He smiled watching his father interact with her. Jerry was wearing his usual formal attire, although he probably thought it was casual without a graceful tie around his neck. Jerry wasn't a stiff or anything; Charlotte said he was just plain British. He used to tell them when they were younger than he had a bit of royal blood in him, called Charlotte his queen and Liza his little princess; the boys, the jesters.

Charlotte was talkative, bubbling with Southern energy, forever ready to cook for a guest, or two, or twenty. She had wavy, very light red hair with a small gray streak on just one side of her part. Jerry called it one moment of calm in a sea of fire. If gray hair represented calm, Jerry's hair was right on the mark.

Shaun loved the energy of his mother but did not know what he would do without his dad. He was the constant. He had a routine every week: work at the Navy base office until 5:30 every week night, cards with Charlotte and their friends every Tuesday where they gambled for pennies, Sunday night steaks, chess with the kids whenever one of them had some extra time, Saturdays for roses, and books between. He was soothing as a rocking chair on a rainy morning. He rarely yelled and could usually find the middle ground as the kids dealt with the challenges of growing up.

Charlotte pulled Shaun out of his thoughts as she plopped down beside him. "I like her."

"Like who?"

"The girl. Annie." She looked sideways at Shaun as he concentrated on taking a large gulp of the sweet tea she had brought out.

"Oh. Well, we've only known her five minutes."

"You going to get to all that work you have?"

Shaun swallowed the last of his glass, wiped his mouth, smiled, and winked at his mother. "I figured we don't help you and Dad as much as we should in the yard. I might do some weeding or be a real man and learn how to prune in a couple of minutes."

"Aren't you thoughtful." Charlotte rolled her eyes, and a matching pair of dimples appeared. "Help your mama wash these dishes first?"

He bent down to scoop up the tray and cups. "Sure, Ma. Thanks for bringing them out to us."

Jerry walked over to the patio and held the door open for the pair, who was gathering crumbs, napkins, and cups from the table.

"Is she getting it?" Shaun asked, looking over at Annie who was bent over, very carefully trimming one of the large, red bushes.

"Oh yes, she's a fast learner. You'll join us, I hope?"

"Well, I don't want to, you know … hang around too much or anything."

Jerry grinned. "Oh, I think you're fine, Shaun. She didn't seem unhappy about someone her own age being around. Now go get those dishes started for your mother so you can teach Ms. Annie about the Japanese beetles."

Charlotte smiled up at her husband as Shaun retreated inside, and Jerry kissed her forehead affectionately.

"Jerry Murray, you're matchmaking."

His eyes twinkled. "I don't know about that. But I'd be lying if I said it didn't cross my mind. And I can't tell you the last time I saw that boy *weeding*."

"You sneaky, little English Yenta," Charlotte said happily. "I believe I'm impressed with your plan."

"Ouch, it's not a plan, love." He pulled her in for a hug before she stepped inside. "Let's just sit back and see what happens."

"Five cents says Shaun asks her out tomorrow."

"You let him do it if he wants to, Char. No pushing it."

She placed a finger to her nose and rolled her eyes again. "Mum's the word."

Annie's hands were dirty, her nose was practically covered in new freckles. Her back was sore from bending over, and her stomach was full of Charlotte's snacks. She was happier than she had been in weeks.

"Are you sure you can't stay for supper?" the red-haired woman asked, helping Annie look around for her purse she had misplaced.

"I'm pretty sure I set it in the garage. Shaun said he'd check there when he put the tools away. And I'm sorry, Mrs. Murray. I'd love to stay but I have to have dinner with my parents tonight. I cancelled lunch on them, so they are driving in for dinner instead. Unfortunately …" she muttered under her breath. "Plus, I've also got to wake up bright and early tomorrow to plant my very own rose bush in my little backyard before I get some studying in."

Charlotte continued to flurry around, talking over her shoulder as she walked into the kitchen to prepare a plate of leftover cookies for Annie to take home. "All right, I suppose we'll let you go this time. And sweetie, you have got to learn it's Charlotte. Mrs. Murray was my mother-in-law, and I swear I'm not that old yet."

Annie grinned, following Charlotte and leaning her back against the kitchen wall near an old cord phone that still hung charmingly beside the doorway.

Shaun poked his head around the corner. "Got it. It was right where you said you left it." He held up her oversized, flower-covered, fabric purse. "I mean, I see how you lose it so easily. It's so small and blends right in ..."

Annie laughed. "You never know what you need and where. But ninety percent of the time, I bet you I've got it in there."

"Oh really?"

"Yes, really."

"Well put these in there in case you need some snacks on the way home or after dinner tonight," said Charlotte, holding out a Ziplock baggie full of cookies.

"I don't know if these will fit," Jerry joined in, coming into the room with a vase full of beautiful budding roses of every color he had.

"Oh, wow!" Annie breathed. She clasped her hands in front of her dirty T-shirt in delight.

"You worked hard today. Take these home; I promise they'll light up the room."

"Wow," said Annie again, gathering the vase into her arms while pulling out her keys from the purse. "Thank you so much. This is just the sort of thing I need in my house."

"Well, thank yourself; you treated my roses very well." Jerry nodded at her, his brown eyes still gentle and kind.

Annie flashed another bright grin, obviously pleased with his approval. She walked out, waving with a couple free fingers and shouting thank-yous and goodbyes as the three members of the family stood on the porch calling their own goodbyes and come-back-soons and well wishes.

Annie put the vase on her table as soon as she got home, still smiling widely. Jerry was right. The colors lit up the room and gave it a beautiful, homey touch. She bent down to complete the picture with a plate of Charlotte's cookies, and her fingers enclosed around a loose scrap of paper

Lunch tomorrow? Come by at 11! –Shaun

It was the messy kind of handwriting, slanted and thin, like her own father's, who was a doctor. Which made her vaguely wonder what Shaun actually did for a living. He presumably lived on his own and worked full time. She herself was almost done with her undergraduate at Lynn Dartin University, one of the few schools in the nation left only for girls, just the way her mother planned since she was little.

Still musing about Shaun, school, and her mother, she hung the note on her fridge and reached for her phone to see what Zoe was doing. She'd eat Annie's day up like French toast for breakfast, powdered sugar and all. Just as she picked up the phone, there was a knock at the door.

Her mother balked when the door swung open. "Good Lord, Annie. You look like the wrath of God. What in the world did you do to yourself?"

Annie sighed. "I was gardening, Mama. And you're here early. Where's Dad?"

"He's on call at the hospital. He'll meet us at the restaurant if he gets off in time." Denise Johnson shook her head. "Please get in the shower, Annie. You smell awful. I could have called a landscaper if I had known you wanted a garden."

"It wasn't my garden; I was learning from someone else." Annie's good mood began to cloud over right away.

"Who is someone else? Do we know them?"

"You don't; I do. It's a family, the Murrays. I met them the other day at the garden shop."

Mrs. Johnson raised an eyebrow. "You went to a stranger's house, Annie? Was that really wise?"

"Mama, they're good people. I promise. Four kids in the family."

Denise balked.

"The oldest is just a little older than me, and the parents are great. Jerry, well Mr. Murray, has this amazing giant rose garden in the backyard; I learned some of the basics of roses today."

"Jerry? First-name basis?" Mrs. Johnson's perfectly painted lips were pursed in disapproval. "I hope you didn't lead with that; I'd hate for you to look ill-raised."

"I'm sure you would." Annie noticed her patience was disappearing rapidly and thought quickly of pruning the rose bushes. Keep the patience, avoid the thorns, clip carefully. "I'm going to get in the shower, Mama."

Mrs. Johnson nodded obviously, and Annie took a deep breath as she turned around. It was going to be a long night.

**

Shaun appeared in his parents' kitchen the next morning. Having some of his mother's cooking talents in his genes, he easily helped make an omelet.

"Over here again?" Charlotte asked. "We just saw you yesterday."

"Tired of me?" Shaun joked, while Charlotte swatted his arm with a towel. Everyone knew when Charlotte was tired of them; they didn't have to guess. She'd holler, "Everybody out!" and had since they were kids. They'd run to the park or jump on their bikes outside. Now that he was out of the house and Billy was working, it had to be a little quieter with just Liza and Brady.

"Anything going on today?" Charlotte asked innocently.

Jerry turned his head slowly to give her a look. *Don't push it, Char,* it clearly said, the corner of his mouth turning up. Her dimples appeared in response, although Shaun did not notice as he rummaged through the refrigerator.

"Might go to the river."

"By yourself?"

Jerry turned again, exasperated. Charlotte ignored him, looking intently at Shaun, who was now digging in the cupboard instead.

"Is there anything wrong with that?" His voice was muffled by the cabinets.

"Not at all," Jerry said pointedly.

"Ma, can you help me make chicken salad?"

Jerry watched the pair, one well over six feet and the other barely over five, bending over a bowl mixing the ingredients together, picking on each other. He had always loved Sunday mornings in the kitchen.

Liza thudded down the stairs later, freshly showered. "What are you doing here?" she bluntly asked Shaun.

"Cooking. Are you allowed to be awake? It's not even noon," Shaun asked jokingly to the second-youngest of the brood.

Liza rolled her eyes in the way only sixteen-year-olds can. "Don't worry; I'll nap like five times today. Life is exhausting with mono, dude. What are you cooking? It's got to be for a girl; you don't smell as bad as usual."

Shaun flicked a grape at her. "We'll just have to see, won't we?" Then he dodged out of the kitchen with his bowl of chicken salad, yelling his thanks as the doorbell rang.

**

"Where are we going? I'm sure your mom could cook better than any restaurant in Maple Falls," Annie inquired as they drove off in Shaun's pickup truck.

"Well, I suppose you'll just have to see," Shaun replied, grinning at her as he pulled to a stop at the first traffic light. "Curiosity killed the cat."

"I'm not a cat, first of all, and I'm a dog person anyway," Annie responded to Shaun's smirk.

He smiled again and reached for the radio to turn up the music. CCR was playing "Bad Moon Rising." ... *there's a bad moon on the rise* ... Annie hummed along and then

61

snickered to herself. Shaun turned to look at her. "What?" he asked curiously.

"I mix up lyrics a lot," she admitted. "And I used to think this song was about a bathroom on the right."

Shaun laughed out loud. "Solid lyric mix-up." He turned it down so he could hear her better. "Did your parents listen to old music like this much?"

Now it was Annie's turn to laugh out loud, although it had a hint of sadness in it. Music was not played often in their house. Her mom would firmly tell her to turn that god-awful noise down when Annie's music got too loud. Annie loved going to friends' houses where parents played all sorts of music and kids were allowed to leave the radio going. As soon as she had a car to herself, she played music constantly, letting the different songs roll through her, filling up those starkly quiet places within her that had longed for sound.

The truck bounced along as Shaun turned onto a gravel road and left the smooth asphalt behind. The road wound into a canopy of trees that sheltered them from the sky's gaze. It was quiet, only a handful of cars went by them, and the drivers put up friendly hands to wave in passing. Shaun would nod and raise his hand to return the greeting.

"You know, it's kind of unusual for me to be driving off with a stranger, having no idea where I'm going," Annie said, almost to herself. "My mother would have a fit."

Shaun made a face at her, drawing one lip up and baring his teeth. "Am I too shady for this?"

She laughed and shrugged. "You could be."

"Fine." He sighed good-naturedly and nodded toward the back two seats to reveal his plot.

"We're going on a picnic?" Annie's eyes lit up, seeing the wicker basket full of Tupperware and an old folded quilt.

"Yes, ma'am. The shady stranger is taking you on a picnic."

She sat back in the old seat that was decorated with ink marks and worn tears in the fabric, and she smiled inwardly. She let her arm hang loosely out the window, the wind pushing gently past. They drove along in comfortable silence, letting the music and the air rushing past excuse them from conversation. Spring was just starting to pop; that light green hue that just whispered of hope was taking over the dreary brown and gray. Some yellow forsythia splashed in random spots where there was a lot of sun, and a few early wildflowers traced the road on either side. But mostly it was a bright green, green, green, alive all around them as Shaun pulled into a small gravel parking lot leading to an area that overlooked the river.

"This place is in Maple Falls?" Annie questioned, gazing at the river stretching before them over piles of mossy rocks and boulders, gently rolling hills unfolding backward toward the horizon.

"Yep. Well, right outside it. Dad and Ma used to take us here when we were kids."

"I've never explored this far," said Annie, realizing just how much of a bubble she let herself live in sometimes. "It's gorgeous."

Shaun's ears turned pink as he smiled, a sure sign that he was pleased. "Yeah, it's not that well known except by locals." He eyed her taking in the scene. "I take it you didn't grow up here?"

She shook her head and tucked a loose strand of curly hair behind her ear. "Not really. I lived in Ralding, which is only about an hour's drive from Maple Falls, and went to the private school there."

"Do you like it? Maple Falls, I mean," he asked, turning to the truck and pulling out the old blanket. He pointed the way to the clearing where they were headed. Their sneakers crunched on the gravel lot, grayish film dusting the edges of their shoes. Annie picked up the picnic basket and, feeling

63

like she was part of an old country painting, strolled side by side with Shaun.

"Yeah, I do, thankfully. My parents wanted me close by. They thought it was a great fit academically, liked that it was all girls, and didn't really want me some place where they couldn't come up every Saturday for lunch."

Shaun noticed a shadow pass over her face as she spoke, like a light had just dimmed behind her eyes.

"But they let you get your own place?" he questioned, looking for a positive.

She shifted the awkward basket to her other hand as they neared the clearing. "Yup! The residence halls were fun for the first few years, but Zoe and I were ready for our own spot this year. Since I knew I was going to be here for the summer, too, for this internship in town, I convinced them it was good for my future. So they let me." She paused for a moment. "It's kind of embarrassing how controlling they are at times."

"Hey," said Shaun lightly. "Every family has its quirks. It's nothing to be ashamed of."

"Yours seems wonderful."

They had reached the clearing, and Annie set down the basket to help him spread the blanket. It flew up into a billowing parachute before they lowered it gently onto the grass. She could smell the laundry detergent from the sheet mixed in with the fresh grass around them and kicked off her shoes so her feet could feel the ground. The sun glinted off her toenail polish, and she wiggled her toes to watch the beams' direction change as Shaun started to set up the basket's contents around her.

"Oh, they're great," he answered, plopping down and pulling out a few paper plates and silverware. "But Brady annoys the hell out of everybody; I mean, he's fourteen. The kid can't help it. Liza is a sixteen-year-old girl, and she and Mom fight over everything—who she's dating and what she does after school all the time. Billy threw everybody off by saying he didn't want to go to college yet and is taking a year off to work and see what he actually wants to do. Wants to study physics eventually, I think?"

Shaun took out the chicken salad and handed it to Annie, who began spreading it onto the bread from the basket. She tossed him an apple, which he caught and took a crunching bite out of before continuing. "And I'm the oldest. I wanted to write, so I majored in English and Business in college. I somehow wound up in construction though, and it works for now."

The project manager job the company had offered him after working most summers there wasn't the worst gig right out of college. He knew he needed to build a savings before he took on any sort of writing projects as a serious pursuit. "I studied abroad for a year in school in Edinburgh, and man, would I love to travel more one day. It just takes time and money, something a college grad isn't rolling in just yet."

Annie smiled knowingly. She noticed how close they were sitting on the blanket together, not quite touching, but butterflies overtook her stomach regardless. The birds chattered loudly in the trees beside them, and every once and awhile, a refreshing breeze rolled in right off the river. "I've only been to my grandparents' in Cape Cod. It's pretty, but not exactly the kind of traveling I want to do. Plus, it's so boring when you're the only kid. You're so lucky to have brothers and sisters," she voiced, shaking her head in jealousy. "Do you fight much?"

"Oh god, yeah," he answered, sitting forward and brushing crumbs off his hands. "I'm personally amazed we're all still alive. Billy and I used to shoot bottle rockets at each other 'til Ma told us she'd take away our bikes for a month if we did it again." He chuckled as he pulled out a bag of chips, offering them to her first. "You don't have any siblings?"

She shook her head and took a sip of one of the water canteens.

"Hmm," he said neutrally. Best not to dig about family it seemed. "So, any ideas as to what you want to do with your life?"

Annie went blank for a moment. No one in her family had asked her that before. When professors or teachers asked, she typically said what she knew she *should* say. Zoe was the only one who Annie truly let her hair down with, mostly because Zoe was always dreaming up big plans and it was hard not to get swept away with her. She found herself sharing this honest answer with Shaun, as they compared friends, stories, and college experiences, classes they liked, and the dream of exploring.

"My internship is actually at the travel agency in town this summer," Annie said. "I should be able to use my marketing classes, but I'm secretly hoping to figure out a way to sneak a trip out of it somehow without my parents realizing it's for fun." God forbid she do something *just because.*

"Tell you what," Shaun said, reaching out to pull her up for a hike along the river. He didn't let go of her hand, and she didn't pull away either. "If you haven't planned a big adventure by this time next year, find me. We'll plan one together."

The corners of her mouth turned upward, slowly and shyly, unable to pull away from those blue eyes. Finally, the both of them turned and grinned at the blue sky that smiled right back.

Down on Priscilla Lane, Jerry reached into his pocket and handed a nickel to a smug Charlotte before he set a vase of blooming roses on the table.

Chapter 9

Annie went home infatuated. She felt giddy and found herself smiling at arbitrary moments, remembering the picnic, the hike, the long kiss they had shared on the trail when they stopped to look at the view. "Don't get carried away; don't get carried away," she told herself. She read her highlighted notes twelve times before she realized she hadn't retained any of the information. She was grateful her friends weren't involved in this relationship yet, no one else to analyze or predict what would happen with her crush. This one felt different.

She took a lawn chair out into the yard, where she sat with a pile of books and watering can while the temperature crept up. After watering her rose bush four times in one day, she decided to swing by the Murrays' to get Jerry's advice to buy more flowers before she over-cared her one measly rose bush right out of existence.

Charlotte answered the door, beaming and thrilled to see her again. "Hey, darling! Come on in! Jerry's outside having a smoke." She pursed her lips. "I can't get him to quit. Here, take some strawberry lemonade with you."

"Thanks, Charlotte. I'll go say hi."

She stepped out onto the patio and waved to Jerry who was sitting comfortably in an old chair. He gestured to the seat beside him, and Annie took it. He put the cigarette out politely. The evening was serene, and she felt no need to speak until the summer air was ready for human voices.

"Lovely evening," he said quietly after she had settled in. His pleasant tone blended right in with the air around them. "Glad you could join us here."

"Thanks, I'm in a lull for schoolwork right now, so I figured I'd come by to get some ideas from your garden to steal."

Jerry tsked. "Gardeners don't steal; we share and are happy to do so." He began to point out the different plants he had around the yard, naming each one, explaining what conditions it grew in, what made it lovely, what made it difficult, and Annie nodded, trying to make a mental note of all of them.

The screen door slammed, and Charlotte came out with a bottle of wine. "Ahhhh," she breathed. "I tell you what, I love summer. The crickets start chirping, the temperature is perfect, and the air is alive with the smell of roses. I'm going to grab a glass of wine; anyone want to join me?"

Jerry took the bottle from her. "You sit; you've been moving for hours. I'll get your glass." He came back out with multiple glasses, humming a song.

"I thought that was your car," said a familiar voice behind her. Annie tried not to let her heart beat faster, but she couldn't hide a grin as she turned around to greet Shaun. She knew she had been hoping he might swing by his parents' house too.

"Hey there," she said.

He held up a box in reply. She squinted to read what was on it. "Chutes and Ladders?"

"My personal favorite board game. Do you have time for a quick round or two?"

She glanced at her watch, although she knew her answer was yes.

"Dad," Shaun cut in. "Has anyone ever mentioned you are a horrible singer?" He shook his head as Jerry started up a Beatles song, ignoring Shaun.

"Ouch, Dad!" Liza chimed in, arriving at the patio. "Shaun's right. Just because you're from England doesn't give you Beatles rights, man."

Jerry stopped and raised his eyebrows. "I am thoroughly offended, young lady."

She laughed and turned to Annie, ignoring her father's comment. "Hello again! Did y'all have a good lunch the other day?" She had a mischievous dimple that matched Shaun's and Charlotte's, but she looked more like her dad, dark hair and features, with a longer, thinner face.

"It was great, thanks," Annie answered, smiling back.

"Hey, hey!" hollered Brady from inside. "Let's play inside, Shaun. It's getting dark out. Some of us actually have a life and want to go out with friends later."

"One week 'til I have a life again; darn mono," mumbled Liza. "I'm never kissing anyone again," she whispered in a conspiratorial voice to Annie, who was too surprised to answer but was pleased to be trusted by Liza.

The group began a hectic game of Chutes and Ladders. The boys were competitive and loud, every once in while getting in a wrestling match to rally against a little too much smack-talk. Annie and Liza rolled their eyes and laughed with the boys, and Annie once again felt more at home tucked in the Murrays' back den than she did with her own family.

Looking down at her watch, she gasped, "Oh my gosh! It's 9:30! I'm meeting some friends, but ... hopefully see you again soon?" she asked.

"Hey, come back and play any time!" Brady said, waggling his eyebrows, clearly approving of his brother's interest.

"Yea, please do," added Liza. "It's nice to have another girl around for a change!"

69

After promises of returning and talking smack for the next game, Annie walked out with Shaun to her car.

"Any of your friends like live music?" he asked.

"Yeah, actually," answered Annie, raising her eyebrows.

"Want to … like … combine friends and hang out maybe? I'm curious about your world," he said almost shyly.

Annie grinned. "I don't know if you can handle my best friend, Zoe. She's a trip."

Shaun shrugged. "Only one way to find out."

**

The spring began to unfold in a natural way, surprising Annie with the ease with which she and Shaun's lives began to overlap. They fell into a routine of meeting after work and class for movies, cooking dinners, board games with his family, playing cards in the quiet of one of their houses, or nights of dancing out with Zoe and their friends. They traded stories, hobbies, and many late nights, leaving toothbrushes and clothes at each other's houses as they went back and forth between them. The more time that went by, the more she found that when she was with him, the tightness in her shoulders eased. He gave her this spark, this feeling of more—wanting more, doing more, living more.

Annie continued to help Jerry in the garden, swapping ideas and plans. Sometimes he'd call Shaun over as Annie worked and he would get her to teach him, as she caught on faster than any of his kids ever had. Charlotte snagged Annie when she could to help her cook meals, and as they baked, they'd talk about books and social issues and Charlotte's favorite friends down at the soup kitchen where she volunteered.

"This one's a keeper," Zoe whispered to Annie more than once. "I mean Shaun's great, but his family is like, half the fun of it."

Graduation came and went. Annie went to the obligatory fancy dinner with her parents, then rushed to Shaun's for a cookout, complete with games, terrible karaoke, and too much to drink. Too many cocktails in her system had Annie leaned up against Shaun late at night, where she shook her head and giggled to him, "I just love you." The next morning, he brought a large coffee, her favorite bagel sandwich, and a note that said, "I love you too." Never had a hangover headache felt so good.

Annie began her internship at the travel agency and enjoyed filling her days with learning the logistics of the business. She and Shaun were growing together, but she was also growing into herself. She told Shaun all the details and her plans for the future, becoming happier and surer as time passed. One day a bouquet of fresh roses was delivered by an eye-rolling Brady, and the women at the agency grinned knowingly when Annie's face lit up. Another day, Shaun raced in on his break with a strawberry milkshake—her favorite. He randomly left notes underneath her windshield wipers, the messy handwriting making her day. She hung every one on her refrigerator.

Jerry and Charlotte came to her to find out how to plan a trip to the Bahamas for a week in July, and she found them the perfect small island to escape to for their twenty-fifth anniversary. They came back sunburnt to a crisp and praised her skills, bringing her a conch shell and bottled pink sand from the beach. She laid them on her windowsill, completely pleased at her first attempt to organize a trip for clients. So they were a little biased; who cared?

Shaun took her to an amusement park for her birthday, where he dragged her to the highest roller coaster.

"No, no, no!" she protested, giggling madly and wringing her hand from his grip. "I'll die! It's too tall! No, Shaun!"

"Anne Johnson, if you don't get on this roller coaster, you are walking home."

"Better to walk home than get in that stinky truck of yours," she responded with a little fire, firmly refusing.

"*Stinky truck? Stinky truck?* That truck smells of hard work and too much time hanging out with you and not enough time cleaning it!"

Away they went, Annie hoisted over his shoulder, still beating protests onto his back until they reached the front of the line.

"I'm not getting on this roller coaster, Shaun Murray. You can't make me do it," she claimed once he set her down, folding her arms across her chest.

Shaun rolled his eyes. "Fine, you're making me beg." He lowered himself onto one knee, took her hand, and gazed into her eyes. "I can't do it without you. Will you, please?"

Others in the line whooped and hollered. "He's down on one knee, lady!" "Give it a chance!" "You gotta say yes now!"

Giving in, she climbed into the next car with him and squeezed his fingers off as the chains cranked their way upward. "I hate you, I hate you, I hate you," she repeated over and over, her eyes clenched shut.

"I know, I know. But," he said, squeezing her hand, "check out the view."

Even the tallest trees were far below their purple car; her hand eased up ever so slightly. "It's so pretty," she murmured, dropping her panicked tone as she looked at the view of mountains around them.

"You are," he answered. "Now hold on."

It's what she loved about Shaun. Her throat was scratched dry from screaming, her legs just barely worked, and her stomach had cracks in it from laughing so hard. He made her feel free.

They didn't agree on everything, and she hated fighting with him. When Zoe argued with her boyfriends, they would raise their voices passionately, slam doors, and storm out on each other, only to passionately make up later. When she and Shaun disagreed, they both turned silent, giving the cold shoulder until someone broke the silence and offered an olive branch. The days in between were stressful, all their thoughts turning inward, which is never a good place for thoughts to circle aimlessly. Still, they found their way, and by the end of the summer, both were talking about the future more seriously. Where they would live. What kind of house they could buy together. How long until they wanted kids. What size wedding to have. In a little less than a year, she simply knew.

They began to plan a trip across Europe together, saving their money for the plane and train tickets, researching the best hostels, reading books, and making bucket lists. Shaun plotted for the best place to propose, wanting it to be perfect.

Somehow, Annie managed to keep all of this relatively quiet with her parents. She was afraid of how they would try to control it, depending on whether or not they approved. She feared the latter. It was always the latter.

Shaun asked some about them, but eventually gave it the space Annie insisted on. Charlotte begged to meet them—"I'll make 'em my best pie; it never fails!"—but Annie kept the subject at an arm's distance. Her parents were toxic, and she didn't want them near the family she had discovered in the Murrays.

"I don't know," she told Jerry one day, frustrated. She was helping him weed the garden before she and Shaun went bike riding on the local trails. "I love them, but they just expect so much sometimes."

"Like what? Perfect grades? Perfect job?"

"Perfect grades, perfect friends, perfect salary, perfect reputation, perfect life. It's all so planned out with them. They think they know what's best, and a lot of what they say makes sense; it's just so controlling sometimes."

"It's understandable," Jerry said in his calming way. "They're your parents. You naturally feel an obligation to them, and they to you."

Annie sighed again. "Yeah. I know it's been months and I haven't introduced Shaun to them. It's just that they're so judging. Not at all like you and Charlotte." She bit her lip and rocked back on her knees. "And I'm afraid Shaun will meet them and bolt."

Jerry stood next to her in his usual slacks and white button-up shirt. "Shaun lights up for you, not your parents. When you two settle down, you're making your own nuclear family. You create your own world, not theirs, not ours. Your own. Every family has its quirks anyway."

She smiled gratefully at Jerry before bending back to the garden. Shaun had said the same thing on their very first date.

"Speaking of your parents," Jerry continued. "Don't you have lunch with them today?"

"Yeah," she said, not hiding the dread in her voice. "I guess I better get to that."

He leaned forward and patted her hand in his now familiar British way. "Don't worry, dear girl. You and Shaun, this is something special. It will all come around."

Chapter 10

Annie found her mother sitting on the kitchen table when she arrived home. Denise's eyes widened at Annie's dirty state. Cutoff jeans. An oversized T-shirt. A floppy hat that had several straws pointing in different directions. Her daughter's state was a bit much for her to take in at once, and she blinked several times. Taking a deep breath, she tried to smile pleasantly.

"How'd you get in, Mama?"

Denise cocked her head. "We made a spare key, remember?" She smoothed her perfectly ironed skirt and sipped on some sweet iced tea from the fridge. "This is delicious tea, Annie." A rare compliment. "Did you make it yourself?"

"Yes …" Annie looked at her suspiciously.

"I couldn't help but notice all these, er, lovely notes on the door here."

Annie said nothing, looking to Shaun's notes and back to her mother, waiting for her point.

"This young man … Shaun … he seems quite infatuated."

Annie's face turned pink, and she continued to watch her mother's expression for signs, not answering her.

"Is he in college?"

"He's already graduated, a year older than me."

"And what does he do?"

Annie sighed. "Is it really important, Mama?"

Denise blinked again. Was there anything more important?

"Anne, I'm simply asking."

"He's a project manager in construction but hopes to be a writer one day."

Denise couldn't keep herself from grimacing.

Annie's jaw clenched, and her fingernails drummed the counter.

"Were you just with this ... boy? Is that why you were late?"

"I'm not late; you're early," Annie retorted, exasperated.

Denise nodded, backing off. This was an important conversation. The boy would be out of the picture soon enough anyway. She tried a different question. "How is your job going?"

"Great, I love it," answered Annie, relieved for a more neutral subject. "I could actually see myself doing this long term."

Taking another sip of tea, Denise dabbed her lips lightly with a napkin. "There's an amazing business program at TCU, you know. They have a master's program you could get in there, which could get you an interview for any job in the country."

Annie scowled, taken back. "Um, Mom, isn't TCU in Minnesota? That's like a full few plane rides away."

Denise shrugged nonchalantly. "I've been talking with your aunt; you know your cousin Audrey graduated from there, and she's quite successful now."

Annie eyed her mother, trying to figure out what she was getting at. This wasn't making sense. "Mama, if something's going on, just tell me."

"Well." Denise sighed curtly. "If you must know, there's a good hospital up there ..."

"For Dad's job?" Annie asked blankly, fumbling for a clue.

"For me."

Annie stared at her mother. "For you?"

Denise smoothed her skirt again, almost impatiently. "I'm sick, Annie. I have a small but slightly complicated tumor we've just found out is malignant."

"Oh God. Oh no. Oh God. Please tell me you're kidding." Annie's breath quickened.

Denise shook her head calmly. She didn't miss a beat. "The hospital there specializes in this though. They are nationally recognized in the treatment I'd need, and your father and I have been discussing the matter—"

"Why didn't you tell me?" Annie cut in angrily, her eyebrows narrowing. "How long have you known? What kind of cancer is it?"

"Hush, child. You're getting worked up. I'm trying to tell you something important."

Annie bit her lip, looking at her mother, her eyebrows drawn tightly together in anxiety. *Child.* Forever patronizing. Annie felt guilty for feeling frustrated, knowing she should be solely focused on her mother.

"We're moving," Mrs. Johnson stated. "You, me, your father. We're moving to Minnesota."

Annie's jaw dropped. "We can't," she immediately responded. She shook her head, her frazzled hair looking even more so as she ran her hands through it. Her mother did her best to ignore her messy state.

She continued as though she did not hear Annie. "Your father strongly dislikes his job here, hospital politics and such, and has already applied for one at the hospital where I will be treated. He's a well-known doctor, so it shouldn't be a problem," Denise went on, her voice both practical and superior. "TCU is right in the city. It would be perfect for us."

Annie shook her head, trying to clear a deep fog that had settled in what felt like the last two seconds. "But it's just treatments, right?" she stammered. "Why would we need to move? I just switched to full-time from my internship. I can stay here and visit you for the surgery and during the treatments," her words spilled out.

Denise cut her eyes at Annie. "I certainly hope you would put your mother before this ... this little job. I have multiple surgeries, radiation, and rehab ahead of me. Your father will be busy with his new job; I'll need you there with me to get through this. I'll need you, Annie," she said heavily, as if to transfer the severity of what she was saying, not allowing Annie to disagree.

Annie had no response. Nothing. No words made their way out of her mouth.

"I know it's hard, but this was only your college town; you'd be moving soon anyway. It's best for the entire situation. For all of us."

"Hard? Hard? Lord, Mama! This is happening so fast ..." Annie began to pace around the small kitchen, breathing quickly, feeling as though the walls were closing in on her.

"Sweetheart, slow down, you're upsetting yourself over something that we can deal with. You've got to calm down."

Annie started shaking uncontrollably, her hand reaching out to grab the counter to steady herself. Her fingers grappled in the air and caught onto the windowsill. They shook so hard as she tried to grab it more firmly that her wrist knocked the bottle of sand Jerry and Charlotte had brought back. It shattered, and pink and white sand burst onto the floor. Annie let out a strangled moan and tried to reach for the broom to clean it up.

"Anne! Sit down!" Denise had leapt up and led Annie to a chair. She kneeled in front of her shaken daughter and wiped a tear that had fallen across a freckled cheek. Her voice was patronizing, making Annie feel like a child again. "It will be all right. They'll fix this, and we'll start anew in a wonderful new city. We've moved before, darling; this one won't be so bad. Think of the opportunities!"

"Mama, I can't leave. I'm so sorry you're sick, and I want to be here for you, but I can't just uproot my life," said Annie, her voice sounding desperate. "Everything is falling so perfectly into place right now. I'll fly up and visit you every weekend. I'll use my savings. I'll support you all the way, Mama, please!" Her sentences ran together, and she began to cry as Denise shook her head. "Your father is constantly working. You know that. I need you there. Your future won't be in jeopardy at all, my dear. Your options will be even better! You see how we're looking out for you, even in such a time for myself?" Denise noticed Annie's eyes glance toward the refrigerator door. She took her daughter's chin and forced those green eyes to gaze into her own.

"He's just a boy, Annie."

Annie let out a sob. "He's not, Mama. You don't understand."

Denise took a deep breath and continued to speak firmly. "Some things are not meant to be. And a small-town boy working in construction? Please." Denise almost laughed. "You can do better, Annie. Think of the men in the city."

Annie's eyes flared through her tears. "You don't understand! His work is valuable! And he's wonderful; he's perfect, I swear. He's smart, ambitious, and responsible."

Denise looked at her doubtfully, as though Annie was a child who just didn't understand. "What is his position?" she asked patiently.

"Project manager. He's a project manager," Annie said, knowing that no matter what Shaun did to make his job successful, this response would not satisfy her mother.

Denise smiled regretfully, though the smile did not reach her eyes. "You don't want to marry that," she said, flipping her hand. "Construction is a hard life, sweetie. It's blue collar. You deserve better."

Annie shook her head furiously, tears still running down her cheeks. "Mama, I love him. I really do."

Denise patted her leg. "It's easy to think that, dear. Let it sit for a little while. You'll see it's not so bad. I've paid the last month's rent on your house today. Movers will be coming for your things. The decision is final, Annie. Now is not the time to be selfish."

Annie put her face in her hands, and Denise continued in her soft patronizing voice, "Stay with him till we move, if you please, but we need you more right now. Your family is most important. We are forever. Boyfriends are not. It will have to end with this boy."

She brushed more salty tears off of Annie's cheeks. "Go wash your face now; we'll leave for lunch soon. I need you to be strong."

Annie nodded blankly. Her eyes felt dry, and her head felt empty. Only the roses she saw from the bathroom window as she splashed cold water on her face seemed to still have color.

That night, she went to the Murrays' as usual and tried to put on a happy face. She told herself she'd break the news later. She couldn't tell them tonight. Not yet.

But everyone noticed that the light was not in her eyes that night, and they all tried to go out of their way to accommodate this change. Charlotte gave her an extra scoop of ice cream for dessert, Brady joked extra, Liza rubbed her back sympathetically, and even Billy gave her an extra squeeze after they said grace around the dinner table. Jerry and Shaun simply watched her, trying to read what had happened.

After dinner, Shaun took her to the rose garden, and they strolled through it, hand in hand. They listened to the crickets sing their song, not needing to talk for minutes upon minutes, simply content with each other.

"Annie," Shaun began softly. "What's up?"

She shook her head, a lump rising in her throat. If she started to talk, she knew the tears would come again.

"Is it your parents?" he asked in a careful tone.

She nodded.

Shaun took a deep breath. "You want to talk about it now or wait?"

"Wait," she whispered.

He squeezed her hand before letting go to pick a white rose that was in full bloom. He handed it to her. "Look at me."

Her green eyes, brimming with tears, turned to his blue ones.

"I'm in love with you," he said firmly, holding her gaze. "That's never going to change." Her tears welled over, and he pulled her close. She could hear his heart—*ba dump, ba dump, ba dump.* "Let's not worry about it tonight, okay?"

She nodded once more.

"Come on, you." He smiled, yanking her arm as he pulled her toward the garage, wanting to do nothing but distract her from whatever was going on at home. "Let's do something. Let's go fishing."

She laughed, tension leaving her body, to her amazement. "Fishing? Where? It's nighttime now."

"Same place we had our first date," he replied, grinning back. "We'll grab two poles at my house, some bait, and go fishing."

She laughed again, and he sighed with relief at the ringing sound.

"How will we catch anything?" she asked, walking quickly to keep up with him. "We can't see."

"Now who do you know that goes fishing to actually catch fish? Besides, you don't need to see a thing; you just wait to feel the pull."

Later, in lawn chairs under a blanket of undimmed stars, she leaned her head against Shaun's shoulder. He kissed the top of her head, nuzzling her in a way that made her feel safe, though she knew the sweetness of the night was a band-aid, that she was being a coward by turning from the broken path that lay ahead, one way or another.

Chapter 11

Annie continued to avoid the subject for weeks after her talk with her mother. She knew it wasn't fair to Shaun, but she did not know how to tell him or the rest of the family. She knew she had something special in her hands. She thought of when they had gone hiking in the nearby mountains, taken road trips to the cities nearby. She thought about the time they joined Jerry and Charlotte for a poker game—the youngest couple by decades. She thought about teaching Liza how to drive stick shift. She thought of the ice cream dates, restaurant dates, and the movie nights in their houses, curled up on the couch with popcorn. She thought of the trip they took to visit Zoe for Mardi Gras in New Orleans, where she had just moved, the beads heavy on their necks as the parades went by. She thought of tending to the rose garden together. She thought of the nights they spent sleeping side by side, and the nights they didn't spend sleeping.

Planning their trips, Shaun wrote stories about the places they wanted to go and gave them to her. He promised that one day, they would visit them all, and go back to all of their favorites with their children. She had felt a sense of belonging and home with him, more grounded and rooted in the world than she ever had, and every day reinforced that. Now it all felt as though it was slipping through her fingers, and she struggled to hold onto it all.

"You need to talk to me at some point," he told her, feeling frustrated and shut out, though he was trying to be patient. "I know something is bothering you. You can't keep hiding it from me."

She nodded. "I know. Not yet, though, Shaun."

**

She went to Jerry first; she knew he would be soothing and help her find a way to tell Shaun. She waited until they were pruning one afternoon in the garden, as they so often did on weekends.

"My parents are making me move to Minnesota," she said suddenly.

His eyes widened for a moment, and he took a deep breath. "Oh wow. That's what's been on your mind."

She let out a small, humorless laugh. "Yeah. You could say that. We're leaving in a matter of weeks. My mom has cancer. She and Dad looked for the best hospital to treat it, and there's this one up north she needs to go to." She pulled through the leaves, checking for beetles to flick away, barely able to look at Jerry. "Apparently, they've been wanting to move, too. And didn't tell me. And now that she's sick and needs a good hospital and follow-up care, they decided this was the spot."

Jerry let out a breath. "I'm sorry to hear about your mother."

Annie bit her lip again. "She said she needs me to take care of her."

Jerry nodded, letting her continue at her own pace.

"There's a good school up there. I'll take the next few months off from work to take care of Mama and apply again to go to TCU for the business program." She looked up at Jerry as a small tear escaped her eyes. "I want to stay, Jerry, I really do. But my family needs me right now. I can't let my mom fight this on her own. She drives me crazy, but I can't just desert her for my own wants right now."

He rocked in the patio rocker, steady and calm as ever. "We would never expect you to, my dear. We'll miss you terribly, but your mother is indeed most important right now. Minnesota isn't too, too far away."

Annie swallowed and took a shuddering breath, finally sitting down across from Jerry on the patio. "Mama doesn't want me to be with Shaun right now. She said family needs to come first."

"Ah." Jerry inhaled deeply, head tilted back in understanding. "I see. And what do you want?"

She shook her head. "Of course I want Shaun, but I also can't leave my family hanging. There's no good answer here. And I just don't know how to tell Shaun that I can't say no to my mom right now."

"Just be honest, Annie." Jerry shrugged simply. "That's the only thing you can do right now. We know life is messy. Shaun will too. Have a little trust in each other." As he spoke, Charlotte quietly came out of the back door, scooching Jerry over to sit beside him. Jerry nodded at Annie, giving her the courage she needed to share what was going on with Charlotte, whose face displayed every emotion in her system like a book.

"Oh, Annie, no wonder you've been out of sorts lately. You need to talk to Shaun, sweetie. We're all fine and good to process with, but he's the one you need to sort this out with," she said, holding onto Annie's hand, the warmth of her small hands transferring to Annie's.

"I wish it wasn't so hard," Annie murmured, and seeing the easy way Charlotte and Jerry simply fit together, moved together, spoke together, she felt a pang that she would never have someone to grow old with. "I wish it could just be like you two."

Jerry cocked his head as he and Charlotte looked at each other, a knowing glance that held many years of marriage within it. "Well, our path hasn't exactly been easy," he said with a slight laugh. "No one's is. If they say it's easy, they're lying."

Charlotte nodded truthfully, her face frank. "Love doesn't translate to easy, baby girl," she said. "There were days raising four kids and running my own business when I didn't even want to look at him, feeling exhausted and resentful. Or I'd feel like his work still took precedence over the work I was doing. We had fights, yelled things we didn't mean, felt broken and worn down."

Jerry looked back at Charlotte, acknowledging this struggle with a squeeze of his hand. "I had to learn about balancing a family with my job, and that was a learning curve. We had to learn what worked and what didn't. We still do."

Tipping her head backward to face the trees and skies above them, Charlotte sighed. "I've been in some dark places mentally. Fighting to stay afloat, to keep perspective, to keep going. Depression runs in my family, only we didn't talk about it when I was growing up. I had to learn to face it, and it took me some time. Jerry had to support me when I wasn't emotionally there for anyone for a while. Just stuck. Just sad. Turning to compulsions as my outlet. Making our life more strained. It wasn't my finest moment as a mother, or our most glamorous marriage memory, but it's real life. All of it—even those rough, rough years—is a part of our story." Coming out of her thoughts, she leaned toward Annie. "Love isn't easy. Life is messy. Perfect doesn't exist. You just gotta talk to Shaun."

Annie nodded, the lump still rising in her throat. "I know."

85

Chapter 12

Shaun was just finishing a report when a woman stepped into his building company's office about two weeks later. There was something familiar about her frame and the way her face was shaped, and he glanced at her for a minute as she looked around.

"Mrs. Johnson?" he questioned curiously.

She turned to him, taking in his shirt and worn jeans with a cold look. "You are Shaun, I presume?" she asked, her tone superior and wary of him. Shaun immediately understood any issue Annie had with her parents.

"Yes, ma'am. Shaun Murray. It's nice to finally meet you," he said as pleasantly as he could, holding out his hand.

"I'm not here for small talk," Denise Johnson said, her tone icy and firm. Shaun dropped his hand. "Perhaps Annie told you of our situation?"

Shaun didn't say anything and kept his eyes directly focused on hers. He was glad the beautiful green in Annie's did not come from this woman. He remembered Annie's tears that night in the garden, and his eyes narrowed.

"We're moving in a week," Denise said simply.

He looked at her blankly, taken back. "Moving?"

"To Minnesota. Annie's coming."

"Um, she's an adult who can make her own choices, right?" he asked, his jaw clenched silently, the only outward sign of deep distress. His stomach, however, had flown rapidly into a thousand knots. *Moving? Annie was moving?*

"I have cancer, Mr. Murray, and I'll need her. She would not desert her family nor disobey my wishes." She looked over him smugly. "Clearly, she has forgotten to mention this whole thing to you. You must be an important part of her life," she said sarcastically, with an unusual ability to make others feel small.

Shaun remained silent. His mind raced, struggling to find out where he had fallen behind before he could even start to catch up.

"We won't be returning, Mr. Murray," Denise went on, looking straight into his eyes. "And you'd do well not to follow my daughter."

"Annie may want to obey your wishes to help you," Shaun replied slowly and cautiously. "Fortunately, I feel no need to do the same."

Denise smirked at him. "What if they are Annie's wishes too?"

Shaun's crawling insides froze. "What? There's no way ..."

"My daughter and I have discussed this weeks ago. She is obviously afraid to break any of this sad news, but we agreed that when she left, a boyfriend would not be appropriate."

Seeing the anger and confusion cross his face, she continued, "She said herself she is not ready for a relationship of this nature and she knew all along that this was not forever. She assured me it would be over when she left for Minnesota. I had assumed she had already talked this through with you as well."

"You're lying," he said. This was ridiculous.

"Tell yourself that all you want, Mr. Murray. But why has she not told you of the move? Tried to convince you to follow? Expressed her undying love? I'm sorry she was not honest with you, but I am here now to ensure that you understand the situation." She kept eye contact with him, holding her clutch close, as though she didn't want to get too close to anything in the office.

He simply glared at her, his heart pounding. "Have a nice day, Mrs. Johnson," he said curtly and walked out of the building, his mind going in one thousand directions. His throat was tight, and his heart was feeling as though it was a stone thrown into his stomach.

**

Annie heard a knock on her door and stood up quickly, relieved to have an excuse to stop packing. Only a week left. She had to tell Shaun. She walked through the living room and opened the door. She smiled immediately at seeing him at the door, but her grin faded quickly.

"What's wrong?" she asked him.

His face was red and flushed, his eyebrows drawn in tightly. "Annie, please tell me what's going on." Even. His voice was too even. He sounded as though it was taking everything he had to remain calm and wait for her answer.

Her eyes darted across his face. "Who told you something?" she asked defensively.

"You've been acting weird for three weeks now. I know something is wrong; I'm not an idiot, Annie … I know you, I can tell. Now tell me, what … is … going … on." He stated his last sentence slowly, saying each word separately and distinctly.

When she remained quiet, her heart pounding and totally unready to have this conversation, he stepped past her into the house and gazed around. Brown boxes littered the floor, some half full with books and movies, some with dishes piled in carefully with tissue paper wrapped around them. Others were completely packed and ready, taped up and stacked, ready to go. The brown looked so bland and rough next to her smooth, now empty, walls of bright blues and greens.

"What …" he trailed off, gazing in disbelief. "It's true, then?"

Annie leaned back against a wall hard, putting a shaking hand to her forehead, pushing fraying hair out of her face, He nodded, his jaw once again clenched tightly, holding it so firmly that it hurt his mouth. He didn't care.

"Damnit, Annie." Shaun was still calm, his voice excruciatingly controlled.

"I wanted to tell you. I just … I just didn't know how," she said desperately, her eyes pleading for him to understand.

"Who told you? Did Jerry or Charlotte tell you?"

He blinked once, staring at her. "You told Dad and Ma? Am I the only one who doesn't know?"

Annie let out a small cry. "I'm sorry, Shaun. I—"

Someone knocked at the door again, and she wiped a tear quickly away, swinging the heavy wood open again. Two large movers stood in the doorway.

"You Ms. Johnson?" one asked.

"Uh, yes … can I help you?" she said, looking bewildered. "Did my mother send you?"

Shaun's eyes narrowed again at the mention of her mother. "Yeah, I'm sure she did," he spat out angrily. "Are you ever going to control anything in your life, Annie? Or is she going to determine it all?"

The movers looked down, shuffled quickly by them, and began carrying furniture out to the truck. It scraped loudly as they hollered directions to each other, and the extra noise frazzled Shaun and Annie even more.

"How dare you say that?" she said angrily, trying to be heard over the movers. "She's sick, Shaun! She has cancer! I need to be there for her. Can't you understand that?"

The movers jostled by them. "Excuse me, miss, we'll just step through here."

She and Shaun barely noticed them.

"I just don't see why it means we can't be together," Shaun said loudly over the metal ramp slamming into the street from the truck. The movers continued to bark directions at one another, shuffling furniture and interrupting cluelessly to ask questions.

"I just need to be focused on my family right now! It's months of surgeries and treatments and rehab. I've tried to figure out solutions, a way to make this work. But I don't have a choice right now; I can't desert them."

They were standing a couple of feet apart; she was still backed against the wall, and he stood in front of her. As she spoke, his broad shoulders slumped.

"But you can desert me?" he asked, his voice barely above a whisper.

Her face crumbled and tears leaked out freely, making trails down her cheeks. "Shaun, don't say that."

"Somebody has to, and you're obviously not going to." His blue eyes were full of pain, and she could barely stand to look into them. He blinked furiously, trying to hold back his own tears. "God, was this whole time a joke? Everything you told me a lie? I was ready to propose to you, Annie."

He pulled out a very small box, the kind of small box that, only a few months ago, her heart would have leapt with joy to see. "I had this made before our trip we were supposed to take; it's not much, but out of all we planned for our trip across the oceans, this is what I was most excited about. Asking you to marry me."

Annie's heart froze, and she let out a single shuddering sob, tears starting to pour. Shaun flipped the lid up to show where a simple gold ring with a beautiful small diamond sat, like a gut-punch. "The trip," she whispered in a strangled voice, as if that's all she was grieving. He closed it gently, holding it tight in his hand.

"It doesn't have to be like this. I swear, it doesn't." He stepped closer, where he could see the outline of her eyes. "I'm in this for the long-haul. Tell me you love me. Because really, that's all that matters. We'll figure the rest out together."

She brought those beautiful green eyes up to his, her face torn apart with tears. "I love you, Shaun." She paused and continued, dropping eye contact, grimacing. "But—"

He dropped her chin and turned on his heel, rage and pain and fear pounding through him. He leaned his head against the wall. He heard her sink to the ground and continue crying. The movers walked past again, awkwardly oblivious to the scene around them, cardboard boxes filing out. The coffee table where they had played cards. A nightstand Shaun had built her to hold all of her books. Boxes labeled 'clothes,' 'kitchen,' and 'school' in Sharpie marker. The silence stood between them. It filled the room, ballooning between their bodies. It was heavy and dark. Shaun's chest felt like cement, an unmoving weight upon him.

"What has this woman done to you?"

Annie, eyes puffy and red, managed to glare back at Shaun. "That *woman* is my mother. I need to be there for her right now." Her hands shook, but her voice, choked with emotion, was steady and low.

Shaun turned his face as though he had just been slapped. He closed his eyes, and every moment from the year that he had memorized flashed through his brain: Annie laughing beside him as they walked along a trail, her hair always pulled back, fly-aways framing her flushed face; the first game of Chutes and Ladders where Annie and Liza high-fived any time they got a ladder; her back leaning against his chest as they reached the top of the mountain and gazed out at the view, sweaty but completely satisfied with their success; the smell of her hair after a shower; each note he had scribbled out on his way to work; her soft hands on his as she taught him the art of pruning rose bushes; watching Jerry and Charlotte dancing in front of her on the patio; singing at the top of their lungs in his truck as they plowed down the old country road; the curve of her hips.

Every kiss, every touch, every snapshot of her he had taken in his mind seared through his chest.

"I wasn't lying when I said I'd love you forever," he said quietly, and the tears finally fell.

Her face crumpled again, and he held her hands tightly, leaning forward and kissing her, gently at first, then hard with anguish and want. Barely able to stand the feel of her lips, he broke away and walked out of the door, brushing past a mover, leaving Annie sitting on the floor, her head in her arms, crying as though she would never stop.

Chapter 13

Annie stayed in her house, refusing to answer the phone when her mother or Zoe called, unable to muster the energy to speak. The day before she was due to leave, she got in her car and drove to the Murrays' house. Charlotte answered the door, and seeing who it was, simply held out her arms. Annie fell into them and lay her head on Charlotte's soft shoulder, letting her rub and pat her back, whisper soothing nothings, and smooth her hair. "It's all right, baby girl. It will be all right." She helped Annie brush the tears away and led her into the house. Liza was sitting at the kitchen table and stood up quickly, imitating her mother and going straight for a warm embrace.

"I'm sorry …" Annie started to say.

"Life is complicated," Charlotte interrupted, and Liza nodded, mirroring her mother. "You have enough on your plate right now; don't be worrying yourself more over us." She pointed to the garage door. "Jerry's out back, of course. He was going to go see you today if you didn't come by. To say goodbye."

Annie nodded, still not able to talk for the lump in her throat, and walked outside. She saw Jerry in his attire that never changed, watering the spread of roses. He glanced up at the sound of the door and sighed with relief when he saw who it was. He motioned for her to come over.

She crossed the yard and immediately let him hug her. "I told him," she whispered into his shoulder. "It didn't go so well."

He patted her back. "Life can be cruel, can't it?" he said sadly. "It will all find a way to work out best in the end." He took her shoulders, pulling her back so he could look her in the eye. "I'm sorry for you both, though."

"Have you seen him much?"

Jerry shook his head. "He's buried in work, avoiding, as he tends to do when he hurts." Annie nodded, understanding completely. The arguments they had, which now seemed so small and insignificant, always resulted in Shaun going silent for a few days, stubbornly retreating inward to work through the issue.

"I'll tell him you came by."

She took another deep, shuddery breath, and asked Jerry for one last stroll around the familiar garden, the roses being the one sure thing in her life she could count on to stay beautiful.

Annie drove for a long time that night, not wanting to go home and face the last of the brown boxes that would fit in her car. She was dreading spending her last night at home alone on just a mattress in an empty room, especially after so many nights with Shaun beside her, when the room filled with so much more than furniture. When she finally pulled up to the house around eleven, she walked slowly up the sidewalk, taking in what had become her home. She was pulling her keys out of her purse when she saw a note on the stoop with a single red rose laid on top. Her body seemed to know she was about to send it on another emotional wave of sadness and braced itself. She picked up the rose, taking a deep, deep breath to smell it before she opened the note and began to read the messy scribble.

You are the love of my life. You have been since the moment I saw you.

I know you're leaving. I hate that you are. I can't bear to think of this as the end, when I truly believed you were the beginning of the rest of my life. You are a part of me, Annie, engraved on my heart. If you decide you want us back, I will be here. Waiting, as yours always,

Shaun.

Annie dried the red rose and kept it until the day she found out about his car accident.

Chapter 14

"Where am I?" Shaun asked, head groggy and eyes fuzzy. The walls around him were a soft yellow, and there was a steady beeping beside him. Two figures stood over him, concern on their blurry faces. He'd seen a lot of concerned faces since Annie had left two months ago, but these faces looked downright scared as they came into focus.

"Ma! Ma! Shaun's awake!" a familiar voice shouted toward an open door.

His eyelids fluttered. The faces drifted in and out.

"Stay with us, Shaun. Come on, man, stay with us," a deeper voice said, sounding oddly choked.

"I'm here …" he murmured vaguely. His head pounded, and he reached up to touch it, feeling only bandages. "That's not my hair …" he mumbled.

Another face appeared above him. She had light red hair and a gray streak along the part. She had been crying, Shaun could tell.

"Ma?" he asked.

"Oh God," she breathed. "Thank you, God. Thank you, God," she repeated over and over. "Liza, go get your father. He's getting coffee downstairs. Billy, take the car and go get Brady. Go ahead now. Scoot."

Shaun blinked again. "What happened, Ma?" Her face was fading more into focus. He could now see her features creased in concern, exhaustion showing through bags under her eyes and worry written in every line. But hope was flickering wildly in her eyes, and he grasped and held on to that emotion as she explained.

He had been t-boned at an intersection the day before, a driver speeding through a red light and crushing his truck. His head had slammed against the window and knocked him out immediately. Charlotte and Jerry had been called as soon as they found his ID. The paramedics pulled his limp body out of the car, and one yelled that they couldn't find a pulse, that it could have been fatal. Pale and shocked, Charlotte clung to Jerry, and they climbed in the back of the ambulance. As the vehicle pulled away, its sirens blaring bad news, a reporter rushed to the scene and began asking questions to the witnesses.

"Would you believe someone told him you were dead, and the idiot printed it," Charlotte told Shaun, pulling out the newspaper. He stared at the picture of his crushed truck, which was entirely unrecognizable. He noticed it was dark; it must have been late evening. He wracked his brain trying to remember any part of the day.

"Ma, I don't remember anything ..." he said, shaking his head in dismay.

"The doctors were amazed you lived, Shaun. You needed a few surgeries and about a hundred thousand stitches, I swear. If all you can't remember is that day, you must have had some guardian angel looking out for you, darlin'."

"Do people think I'm dead?"

Charlotte chuckled with only a bit of humor. "No," she answered. "Someone called the paper, and they're printing a correction. You know Maple Falls. It's always something here."

Shaun began to look more around the room, taking in the cards that hung on his walls from friends, a new football from the guys, and a vase full of roses.

"Your father brought those this morning. Oh lord, Shaun, he'll be so glad to see you up. He's been pacing the entire hospital since we got here, wearing holes in the floor from walking them. I've never seen the man so scared. We all were."

Shaun nodded, feeling tired. His eyes rested on the roses. "Annie ..." he mumbled, remembering the last heart-wrenching month since she had left. He groaned softly, and Charlotte reached down and took his hand.

"You gotta let her go, baby," she whispered, tears welling in her eyes. "It hurts me, too, but you gotta move on, son."

Billy, Brady, Liza, and Jerry entered the room, and Charlotte gave him one last pointed look, begging him to try. He nodded tiredly and turned to the smiling faces. Shaun had never seen such looks of relief and realized how afraid his family had been. Wanting to ease any worries they still had, he lifted his hand to wave.

"Hey, guys." He smiled and mustered his strength to return to the world.

**

It took Shaun weeks to regain the strength he had lost in the accident. His hair began to grow back, thicker and darker; the bleached summer hair was long gone, but he was thankful for anything on top of his head as the days turned cooler. He took a leave from work while his fractured ankle and broken left wrist healed, although he wouldn't have minded the distraction. He sat out on his patio to write every morning. His family treated him like royalty for a few weeks before fading into their normal routine. But no one mentioned Annie. Shaun did not speak of her, not even to Jerry. Liza brought it up one afternoon, but Shaun shook his head.

"I can't talk about her. I can't even think about her." He shrugged apologetically. "I'm sorry, Liza. Just please … don't."

Once he was approved for activity, he began to bike to his parents' home daily to water and prune and care for the bushes, keeping the rose garden in top quality. Jerry commended him quietly, not wanting to draw attention, knowing the reasons for which Shaun poured his heart into the garden. Knowing the blooms were a piece of when he himself had tried to find his way through the twisty corners of life, Jerry simply gave him more ideas of ways to help. He watched, and he worried, pulling for his oldest to find his way through.

It had been two months since the accident; Shaun was biking back and forth from work, easing his way back into a building project. He picked up a few items Charlotte had requested from the store, carrying them in a backpack as he rode. When he arrived in front of the house, Charlotte was hurrying to the car.

Shaun hopped off his bike quickly. "What's wrong?" he asked immediately, seeing the look of panic on Charlotte's face.

"Your father is having some chest pains. He just called from the office."

"He needs a ride home?" Shaun asked, his blood pressure rising along with Charlotte's.

"No, we're going to the hospital. Go ahead, get in."

Chapter 15

The doctors were encouraging, reminding Jerry that he was relatively young. They gave a long list of things to avoid, from bacon to burgers to alcohol to smoking to stress. Because his heart issues were serious, they decided to keep him in the hospital for a couple of days to run more tests. Jerry tried to protest but got caught up in a coughing fit that disabled him from speech as the doctors walked out. Shaun went home to bring some pillows and blankets back to the hospital for Charlotte, trying to be helpful, and bounced from the hospital room to the house to check on the siblings. Charlotte, unable to sleep, was relieved to sit beside Jerry as he slept and watch him, soothed by the steady beeping.

   Notebooks and a couple folders were strewn about the room; Jerry asked Shaun to read him his latest essays and pieces, knowing he had been writing recently. His eldest son sat loyally beside him when Charlotte needed to run home, his long body stretched out on a chair, feet propped up on the bed, head back, fast asleep. Upon returning, Charlotte pulled a blanket over Shaun and smoothed Jerry's hair.

"Don't leave me, Jer," she whispered, holding his hand. He stirred and squeezed her hand, the beep of the monitors steadily continuing behind him.

**

Shaun headed down the shiny hospital hall toward the front desk after he got off work. He was worried about Jerry, his stomach tied in knots. Tests had revealed the need for what should have been an uncomplicated surgical procedure, but Jerry's recovery had been rockier than they had hoped. Although Jerry's smile and eyes were warm as ever, the color had faded from his face, and he remained weak, stuck for the past two weeks in the hospital bed.

The kids visited him every day, constantly. They all continued to tell him of their days and what was going on in their lives, showing him good papers from school or bringing a new library book or the last of the roses from the garden. Charlotte snuck in her own heart-healthy cooking with her to the hospital, not trusting their food to help him recover. She and Shaun spent hours with Jerry, Charlotte in the mornings and early afternoons, Shaun picking up after work when his mom went home to be with the others. She often hauled at least one of the siblings back for a visit before bed, but between the bustle, Shaun amused himself by continuing to write while he waited, watching old movies on the room's television when he needed a break.

Shaun had been watching *The Sound of Music* with Jerry when Charlotte left to cook dinner for the rest of the family at home, promising to bring the whole gang back after they were fed. After the two men waved her goodbye, Shaun bent his head over his notebook.

Jerry looked at the top of his steadily growing, thick hair. "Shaun ..." he said softly, his throat hoarse from coughing. His eyes were full of love and pride for his son.

Shaun looked up at him expectantly, their eyes meeting.

"I know you miss her."

101

Shaun's Adam's apple bobbed as he swallowed painfully. He blinked a couple of times, his pen frozen in midair. Finally he nodded, unable to keep his eyes from welling.

Jerry motioned for him to come closer. "Come here, Shaun," he said. He took his son's grown hand in his own as Shaun brought his chair closer to the bedside. "I know you loved her, and I believe with all my heart she loved you, too. You'll never lose all of her. Hold on to those little bits that made her so special, and I promise you, there will be healing at the end of this. You're going to be okay."

Shaun swallowed again hard, holding back the tears that he had not let fall since the day he left a rose on her doorstep. "She didn't want to be with me. That's not love." His voice sounded broken, and Jerry ached to hear the sound of Shaun's pain.

"Family's a strong tie," he said softly. "She's young still. Perhaps she was afraid for her mother, afraid of what would happen if she went against her wishes, especially while she was sick with cancer. Perhaps she needs this time to be sure of herself. Perhaps we will never understand her reasoning. But that doesn't mean she didn't love you."

Shaun shrugged doubtfully, staring into his father's brown eyes. "I just want her back." His voice cracked slightly.

Jerry patted his hand. "Be patient. You may. Time has a way of softening what was once hard, if we let it."

Shaun ran his free hand over his new head of hair, scratching the growing scruff on his chin. "I'll try," he agreed halfheartedly. "But don't worry about me, Dad. You just work on getting better, okay?"

Jerry smiled. "The garden needs me, doesn't it?"

Shaun turned back to his writing. "We all do, Dad," he whispered quietly. "We all do."

**

Shaun woke up early to visit Jerry, as he knew Charlotte had been there until late the night before, and he hoped she was able to sleep in. Shaun knew his dad had been worried about him lately, and he wanted to reassure him that he was okay. He didn't want Jerry facing any more stress than he needed to right now.

"Jerry Murray," he told the nurse at the front desk, checking in as always.

"Upstairs," she answered automatically, knowing Shaun knew the way.

Out of the elevator, Shaun turned down Jerry's familiar hallway, but stopped suddenly, seeing a swarm of scrubs outside of his door. A light was blinking steadily above the door. Quickly, he ran to the room, where, amid nurses and physicians, he saw his dad, laying still on the bed, eyes closed peacefully. His hospital gown was open at the chest, but his monitors cascading with wires were no longer beeping, no longer blinking numbers and stats and zig-zagged lines of life. A nurse, Cheryl, who knew the Murrays well by this point, grabbed Shaun's arm and ushered him out of the room.

"What's going on?" Shaun said, turning back to the room, half expecting to see Jerry strolling out with his black slacks and white crisply ironed pressed shirt, exuding calm as always.

Cheryl swallowed hard and squeezed his arm as she steered him toward a sitting area. "Shaun, I'm so sorry."

His lips pressed together. He tried to stay calm. Nothing good started with the words *I'm so sorry* in hospital walls.

Her kind eyes welling, she sat him down in a chair at the end of the hall, gingerly placing the vase of roses he had brought for Jerry from the garden on a counter. "Your dad went into sudden cardiac arrest. It was fast, Shaun. We called the code, and the doctors did everything they could." She swallowed, as if bracing herself. "He didn't make it, Shaun."

Shaun's head shook back and forth. "No," he pleaded. "No, I was just here last night. He was fine last night. We talked. He was okay; he wasn't even that tired. Please, it must be a mistake." His eyes begged her to tell him it was all a big misunderstanding.

"Sometimes these cardiac conditions aren't predictable, especially with ventricular tachycardia. It's possible his previous issues and the strain from surgery contributed to his heart simply not being able to pump anymore," she explained carefully and calmly, with tears in her eyes, holding his hands.

"So, his heart just … stopped?" Shaun said, his voice cracking on the last word.

Cheryl nodded. "It just stopped," she answered, and her eyes, too, spilled over.

"Let me take you to another room where you can call your mama. I'm going to page the physician to come in right away to speak with you about … what happened. She should be here any minute, as will our bereavement team. You'll be able to go back in the room with your dad if you want, to … say your goodbyes." She paused, seeing Shaun struggling to take it all in. "I'm so sorry for your loss."

Shaun felt his chest close in. He couldn't find air to breathe.

Barely feeling the weight of her hand on his shoulder, he looked back toward Jerry's room, his face twisted with a deep, jagged ache he'd never felt before. He put his head in his hands, and an emptiness settled in his stomach. "He was just here …" he pleaded again.

He looked up to see his mother step down the hallway to find the same scene Shaun had, her eyes questioning, as confused as Shaun was sure he had looked just minutes ago. She ran down to Shaun, her eyes on fire.

"Where's Jerry?" she asked upon seeing Shaun's tear-stained face and Cheryl's comforting but broken expression, her voice panicked. "I'm here. Where's Jerry?"

Shaun met her eyes. "Ma …" he began, the lump painfully large in his throat. He couldn't get the words out. He couldn't say it out loud.

Her face showed that she registered what had happened, not even needing to hear the words that Shaun was still forcing out. Her shoulders, tensed and forward moments earlier, fell. She knew. Her breath went out, and her eyes closed. She shook her head. "No."

She ran back toward his room, edging her tiny body in past the nurses and doctors, Shaun following closely behind. When she saw Jerry, she froze. It seemed like the whole world did.

"Ma," Shaun quietly wept beside her, "we lost him." Charlotte slumped against the wall, her entire body beginning to shake with loud sobs. Shaun tucked his mother's small shuddering body into his arms. He didn't know how long he stood there, tears pouring silently down his cheeks. Charlotte's tiny hands gripped Shaun's T-shirt, clinging for comfort. He held her shoulders, which jerked with each trembling breath, in a tighter embrace. Shaun opened his eyes and saw the vase of roses Cheryl had gently set inside the room, and he suddenly felt as if his heart had been ripped in half and would never be healed again.

Chapter 16

Shaun asked to speak at the funeral; his siblings gladly obliged, all too shocked to begin to pull together their thoughts about their father. Liza had put together photo collages, old pictures that made them smile and cry at the same time. The gathered folks walked by, pointing at the photos and smiling, dabbing their eyes with balled up tissues. Shaun's eyes raked over all of them; it all seemed too surreal. There was Jerry and Charlotte's wedding photo, awkwardly formal except for their knowing grins. The kids' baby photos with Charlotte and Jerry, the pile of siblings growing with each baby. Riding bikes with Jerry standing near. A sailing trip they took as a family. Christmases. Easters. A hundred ordinary moments that made up a life.

Shaun stared out of the stained-glass window, feeling exhausted, wanting so badly to say the right thing at the service. He listened to nothing the minister said about Jerry at the funeral, gazing at the amazing display of red roses upon the plain pine casket. There had been no question as to what kind of flower was to represent him to the people gathered in the pews. He jerked out of his daze when the minister said his name and motioned him forward.

He cleared his throat and slowly walked to the pulpit. He had written very easily about his dad, but now that he stood in front of his mother, his siblings, and all these people who had loved Jerry and needed solace, his voice froze. Clearing his throat again, he saw the congregation looking on at him with shiny eyes, waiting for his words. When he spoke, his voice was thick. "Calm. Constant. Soothing. Dad was soothing," he began. "He always had a moment for you to stop and share a piece of your life, whether it was a good grade you got on your paper, a story about a friend, or some amazing play you did in football. He was steady, always there. Life was not rushed with him; it just was what it was."

Shaun took a deep breath, looking at his mother for a brief moment, their eyes missing the same man so badly. She looked so small, her eyes puffy but face brave and chin held high. She wore the bright bluebird pin he had given her last Christmas and reached up to touch it every now and then, as often as she would have reached out for Jerry's hand.

"He always wore the same thing. Nice slacks, always ironed, with a good white shirt. Sometimes he really walked on the wild side and wouldn't wear a tie. I don't think he owned a pair of sneakers. Even to work in the garden."

He smiled inadvertently, imagining Jerry bending down in sneakers to pick weeds in the garden. "He grew roses. And roses aren't an easy thing to grow. I think we kind of took the garden for granted until we got older and saw all the work and care he put into it. The roses were gorgeous. He loved springtime because that's when he could start really getting to work out there, working to make those roses bloom. We always used to joke that the number of roses he grew got larger with the number of children who could work on them. Sure enough, by the time Brady got old enough to start yanking out weeds, Dad had about seventy-five bushes in the backyard.

"Every Saturday, we had to go out and work on the roses, cultivating around them to weed and make sure the soil was broken off so water could get in, checking for disease, fun stuff like that. We weren't allowed to use fertilizer to help them grow either because Dad believed in manual labor … or child labor, depending on the point of view from which you're looking."

A few chuckles echoed through the pews, as people remembered visiting the Murrays' house in the spring and summer.

"He always cut roses on Sunday and brought them in for dinner. And like I said, he always worked in the yard in black street shoes, dress pants, and a button-down collar shirt with no tie. Dad's concept of casual was no jacket or tie. I never saw him in sneakers, never in a polo shirt or T-shirt. That was just Dad. Consistent. He was always the steady one, the one that wouldn't get frazzled or upset or unnerved by anything. His demeanor was as solid as the foundation of things. I guess that's why the roses loved him. It is such a finicky and difficult flower to grow and keep alive, but he did it beautifully with his gentle and patient touch.

"Dad's rose garden was his life. I don't mean it took over his life. I mean he lived life like it was his garden. He treated us with such patience and care, even when we were hell to deal with. He was careful and constantly there raising Billy, Liza, Brady, and me, always giving us something to lean and grow on, someone you could always count on. He always had time to spare to make sure we were doing okay. There were always thorns, always weeds and beetles to get rid of, but he always knew how to make the flowers thrive above all. Not only that, but, without even realizing it, he taught us how to do the same."

Shaun swallowed again, missing his father more than ever. "He was so proud of that garden; of his family; of Ma, his partner through it all; of the people he loved. It was something magical to him, and the magic answered back with beautiful blooms that sat on our kitchen table every Sunday night.

"He told me once ... he told me once that if you miss someone you love, you'll never truly lose them if you remember the tiny things that you loved most about them ..." Shaun took a moment to let the wave of pain wash over him so he could go on. He thought of Annie and Jerry laughing in the garden together. Shaun was quiet for several moments, desperately trying to gather his composure. Finally, he went on in a voice that wavered horribly.

"Dad was a gift to each and every person here, a man who brought out the beauty in life, who saw the potential in everyone and brought it out, who was patient and kind when most people would have pulled all of their hair out in frustration, who could bring out the peace in the pickiest flower on Earth. He was a husband, a father, a friend, a gardener in so many ways, planting something within all of us. His garden will truly live on as we hold Jerry Murray near and dear in our hearts."

Chapter 17

After the funeral, Shaun felt as though a fog had settled over him. There wasn't closure. He didn't feel peace. Everyone said, "Your dad is with you," as a comforting solace, but he didn't want his dad's spirit; he wanted the real thing. He felt wracked with guilt for causing Jerry stress. Unable to wrestle with such enormous emotions, Shaun spent hours and hours of the day pruning, weeding, and watering the rose garden. It was the end of October, and almost all the flowers had fallen, covering the mulch in petals trimmed in brown. He took on less at work, and simply wandered through the gardens, through the park, up and down the roads on his bike. His thoughts were fuzzy, laced with roses, the smell of hospitals, Jerry's image in the garden, and brown boxes in a moving truck. There was so much to grieve. Everything reminded him of his dad, and his father's memory would not let him forget the woman in the back of his mind. He had no idea what to do without Jerry's calm, constant guidance— gentle but always there. He felt empty without his reassuring presence. Colors and meaning faded, and Shaun ached with memories that replayed over and over in his mind like a broken record.

The house was quiet; Brady and Liza went to friends' houses often, the distraction and change of scenery helpful. Charlotte methodically went through the logistical processes afterward, tackling each step with a breaking heart but brave spirit. She found healing in openly remembering Jerry, grieving honestly. "Feel the feels, baby," she'd tell her kids, to whomever was having a hard day, missing Jerry. She was strong for the family, but Shaun's insides hurt as he watched her sit on the patio with a Coca-Cola, a sweater wrapped around her in the fall chill, eyes closed and brown leaves drifting to the ground around her. They all looked for ways to deal with the hole that seemed too large to ever fill. Charlotte turned outward and faced her raw grief, but Shaun curled inward, wanting to numb his heart from the sharp pains that persisted.

He could not escape the pain, though. He blamed himself for everything that had happened—for Annie, for his accident, for Jerry. He knew he had put an extra strain on his dad, wondering if that's what had finally made his heart fail. He loathed himself at times, yearning for direction.

"I need to go, Ma," he told Charlotte suddenly one night as she stirred stew slowly on the stove. With all the food in the house, she had started bringing leftovers to a local shelter, prompting her to make large meals and bring them over when she could.

Her sad eyes turned to him. "Go where?"

"I don't know. I need to leave for a while, though. Leave Maple Falls." His eyes begged her to understand. "I'll get a job somewhere else. I need to just do something different right now."

Charlotte gazed at him, knowing her son's aching heart, barely able to deal with her own. "For how long, Shaun?"

He shrugged.

Tears leaked from her eyes. "Oh Shaun … it's going to be okay. We're going to be okay."

"I'm sorry, Ma. It just … it just hurts too bad."

A week later, he was packed and on his way.

111

Charlotte got a letter the next month. It was Shaun's usual go-to of expression, always turning to writing rather than talking. He explained that he felt like everything was his fault, and he was not helping his family at this point. He would miss them terribly while he was gone, but he needed to go for a bit and re-find himself. He said he loved her dearly and could never ask for a better mother, and he would try to do her and his dad proud. He'd keep writing when he could to let her know he was okay. It was signed "With love, Shaun."

**

For the next two years, he traveled around the coast, working construction in different cities, moving multiple times, never able to feel settled where he landed. He wrote a letter home every once in a while at first, stating that he was fine and working, meeting good people, and that he missed everyone back home. The letter his mother wrote him back was sweet and supportive, but it tore him with guilt.

Ashamed, Shaun ran, trying to escape the memories that visited him in every dream. He moved again twice. He visited home once, but felt painfully out of place, the memories that came flooding back nearly crushing him. His mom had started up catering again and seemed happy having an outlet to cook and socialize and laugh again. His siblings had all found things to keep them busy and healing. He stayed only a day before he hit the road, driving even farther this time.

His mom came to visit him once, but he felt so bad about her having to make the drive that he found reasons to postpone future visits until she just didn't offer anymore. He convinced himself that his family was better off without him and his stalemate lifestyle; checking in continually would just make things worse, and they would only be disappointed if they knew what he was doing with his life—or not doing, if he was honest with himself. Little by little, he built a solid wall that grew to hide his past. The more guilt he felt, the more he hid behind the wall.

Shaun threw himself into work, mostly construction, and months passed by. He thought less and less about the world he had left behind so long ago. He was out with a group of the guys one night when they decided they needed a midnight snack. They pulled their heavy trucks into a pancake house and got a booth. They all grinned eagerly when their waitress brought out their menus, smiling sweetly at the group of men and asking for their orders. Shaun was captivated by her high cheekbones and tempted by the sway of her hips when she walked away to bring the order to the back. She turned as she was walking away, catching his eye and smiling. She laid his plate down last when their order was ready, and the boys laughed when they saw the smiley face she had put in the pancakes with chocolate chips. She grinned, walking away, and wrote her number on the bottom of his check for $7.43.

Eleven months, three weeks, and five days later, Marie was born.

PART III

"Shaun, don't leave yet. I know I screwed up really bad, but don't leave yet!" Olivia said the moment Shaun closed the bedroom door behind the two of them, leaving Marie in the living room with her favorite movie on. Shaun had promised an ice cream dad-daughter date later where he'd explain as much as he could, and she jumped at the deal for a sundae and real grown-up talk.

Shaun gazed at Olivia in their tight quarters, completely bewildered, adrenaline still pulsing strong. "Don't even go there right now, Olivia," he said, shaking his head as a warning. "We've got a whole lot to get through that should have been said about seven years ago."

She nodded knowingly. Shaun was actually surprised at the concern in her black eyes. He had seen a great deal of things pass through those dark windows through which she saw the world. Attraction at first. Since then, anger. Defiance. Indifference. Drunken glares. Exhaustion. Moments of motherhood with Olivia. But this anxiety, concern, fear … never. He decided to wait to address the change. He needed answers.

"You hid this from me?" he questioned, holding the letter up. His eyes were piercing.

She nodded once more and did not hesitate to explain. "Your mother sent it to an old address, and somehow it actually got forwarded here. She had a small note attached." Olivia went on to Shaun's shocked expression. "She said it was your battle, your story to tell this Annie if you chose to. She said she missed you." Olivia's voice broke with the weight of the secret she had held for so long. "She said to come back home. She said it wasn't the same without you, and she worried about you. Everyone, your brothers and sister, sent their love."

Shaun stared at her, fury, hurt, guilt, and pain all squeezing at his chest.

"I wrote her," Olivia continued, unable to stop, her voice still strong as ever, but her face was clearly afraid as actions she had justified in her head years ago were spoken out loud. "I wrote a letter saying Annie was not a part of your life anyone. And that you missed everyone, too, but would be away for a while longer. The letter had come right before Marie was born, and I sent that note back just a couple of days before I went into labor." She gulped, continuing, "I sent Annie one saying your dad had passed away shortly after your accident. That your family had moved away." She shrunk as far as she could into the wall, afraid of the glare in Shaun's eyes at her confession.

"What gave you that right?" he said slowly through a clenched jaw, his voice shaking with emotion. "You have been anything *but* a loving person in my life for these past seven years. You refused to get married; you let me raise our child nearly all on my own; you have brushed this family aside time and time again; you have crawled to the bottom of a bottle instead of to bed with me. Yet you think it's okay to decide my life? Communicate to people you don't even know?"

He brushed away the small voice that reminded him of his hypocrisy. He had decided to not face his old life. He was the one who had never reached out to his family again. He was the one who avoided his grief for years, ultimately repurposing himself for Marie but remaining hidden from his past. He remembered when they had brought Marie home, Olivia hesitantly asked if he would tell his family. "Not yet," he had answered. He wasn't ready.

Still, he shook his head wondrously. "I don't understand, Olivia," he said simply, continuing to ignore his recurring guilt. "You weren't happy. It was like you wanted to *cause* problems, tempt me to leave you. You flaunted that we shouldn't be together. You resented this life," he reasoned out loud, finally spilling his frustrations. "I never quite knew why you stayed, and simply attributed it to Marie and money. It just doesn't make sense."

Olivia felt more vulnerable than she had in years and did not like the feeling. She took a deep breath and tried to let her usual feeling of control come back over her. Her initial panic was fading, but she knew she was walking a fine line. "Shaun, I'm just going to be completely honest, okay?"

He snorted. "What a concept."

Her eyes narrowed quickly. "You want to know the answers? Yes or no?"

Shaun answered in furious silence, his muscular arms crossed. His hands made the ruddy skin on his arms turn white as he gripped them tightly. "Out with it," he finally said in a low tone.

Olivia took a deep breath. In a clear, very matter-of-fact voice she explained that her mom left when she was seven; she barely had any memories of her, and her dad refused to talk about her. "Her leaving, abandoning us and never looking back, broke him. He was angry and never got over it. He turned into a mean drunk and sent us into a pretty bad situation. Almost all the money we had went to his drink. I've waitressed since I was thirteen, illegally getting paid practically dirt until I was old enough to get a real paycheck. But if I wasn't working, Dad got angry. And if he got angry, I got hit. The older he got, the drunker he got, and the angrier he got. He'd be alone all day while I went to school. I'd go to work right after until late. When I got home, he'd yell for my mom. When he saw it was me, he'd throw bottles at me, chase me with his belt, hit me with his fists. It was bad. More than bad. I tried to leave a few times, but I just couldn't support myself yet. And it was always worse when I came back."

Shaun stared at her, his body's adrenaline calming as he listened to her speak. He realized vaguely how little they had shared in the past years. It was like her outer layer, so hardened and weathered, was cracking around Olivia as she spoke, and a very different person was allowing herself to show, crack by crack.

She took a breath and went on. "I didn't have a lot going for me when you came along. I had boyfriends, but none of them lasted too long. You were different. I guess it was that you were decent." Her tone was completely straightforward; she had never been one to sugarcoat things. "You gave me something new I had never seen. But when I got pregnant, I felt like I had screwed up my plan, and I was pissed about it.

"It was ironic, really. After we decided to live together, I was finally able to get away from my father completely. But I felt like I was becoming him. I was terribly angry at you and Marie. I did not want to be a mother in the situation we're in. Poor. Not happy with each other. Both running from pasts. But at the same time, you gave me an escape and protection. And I needed that. So I took it."

She paused. "I know I'm not a great mom. And I thought about leaving." Her voice cracked. "But I couldn't just leave my girl. Not like my mom did. I wouldn't ever do that to her."

Shaun continued to stare at her. His arms were still crossed across his chest, and his jaw was still working silently under his small neat beard, but his eyes were less cold as Olivia continued to talk.

"When I got that letter from Annie, I got scared. I realized we were both hiding from something and that was the only thing that kept us together. If you went back to your old world, I'd have nowhere to go with a baby except the shithole where I came from." Her voice finally broke, and the solid sound of Olivia's frailty was so foreign to him that he felt lost for a moment. He resisted the strange urge to hug her, knowing that wasn't her brand of comfort. So he simply kept listening. "I mean, I've seen guys leave their girls and babies in a heartbeat. All the time. And why would you stay with me?

"So, I lied and put up a wall," she went on, seeming unable to stop now that she had finally begun. Her neck was strained as she pushed out the words. "I put up a wall on one side because I was so angry to be stuck in this life with you and a kid. But I built a wall on the other side because I could not go back to my father with a baby. And I trapped us in."

Shaun leaned his head back against the wall for support. "I'm sorry about your father," he said quietly. "I'm sorry for your whole situation. I'm sorry I never knew of it, that I never asked. It must have been awful growing up like that."

She shrugged, her dark shoulders rising and falling in a small tank top she had been wearing around the house. "Neither one of us shared with each other. I don't mean to blame you."

Silence held the room for a minute. "I messed up," Olivia said quietly. "You do what you need to do."

Shaun stared ahead, the weight heavy on his shoulders. He could leave her. She had been selfish and manipulative. She had lied and used him. He could walk away from the mess right now and create another haunting memory from which he would have to run.

"I need to think. I need to process all of this," Shaun said, rubbing his hair. "Can you watch Marie while I take a walk?"

"Yeah. Of course."

Olivia shakily let out her breath. Now that her walls were in pieces around her, she did what she should have done a long time ago. She called Marie in and opened up her closet, where the pink waitressing dress that she knew Marie loved so much hung, and played dress up with her daughter. Olivia was a little stiff, a little awkward, and not so great at pretending like Shaun was, but with some of her swirling resentment and self-doubt and anger let loose from the track it had held in her brain for so long, she was able to simply try being a mom.

And it wasn't so bad.

Chapter 19

It was the trip to Compass Rose that had sent all the waves into motion. As Shaun walked through the night, he remembered how it unfolded.

Marie begged, and begged, and begged for him to take her to the travel company's office to see what it was like. While he thought it would be pretty boring, he thought they could go check it out, then grab ice cream or something cool around the town while they were there. They highlighted the route on a paper map, Shaun pointing out how the roads wound and wove all the way to the company's address that was listed at the bottom of their faithful brochure; the brochure that had provided so many stories and dreams. The travel company was about two hours from the city. Marie was thrilled, making Shaun tell her stories the whole way there as she stared out of the window. Personally, he was thrilled to get out of the small house and his normal routine and was just as excited about the small trip as Marie.

They had hopped off the bus and strolled down the streets of a small downtown area before Marie spotted the Compass Rose sign and dashed toward it, pulling Shaun close behind. He pushed open the heavy door, watching

Marie step through it, her face glowing with anticipation. He grinned at her, then looked up.

The moment he saw her, his chest froze. He saw his own shock mirrored in her face when she started to welcome them. The words never made it out of her mouth as they locked eyes.

She had matured well; her hair was styled differently, but her skin was still smooth, decorated by the freckles across her nose and cheeks he knew so well. He wondered vaguely if they were the same freckles he had loved ten years ago, or if they were new ones.

She wore a bright shirt that brought out the green in her eyes so that their color was vivid against her light brown skin, dancing as they had been so many years ago. She held a mechanical pencil in her hand and must have been working with a customer on the phone when they walked in, for she had just hung up and finished scrawling something out when she glanced up to say hello. The expression on her face changed from warm and friendly to complete shock.

The beard may have kept some from recognizing Shaun right away, but as soon as her eyes met his, her heart simply dropped, and everything stood still. He seemed taller and stronger, and Annie barely noticed that his rough hands were holding a much smaller one, which belonged to a small girl. She couldn't bring her eyes away from him.

He was alive.

His face was weathered, and simply by looking at him, she knew he had been through a great deal. His hair was shorter than the shaggy college-kid look he had years and years ago. The rusty beard on his chin was very short, and she could still see the strong, square jaw underneath. There was a thin scar that wasn't there before, starting on the side of his forehead and into his hairline, but otherwise, he looked so much the same.

She just stared at him before her voice began to work again. She blinked twice, trying to step back into reality.

"I thought you were dead," she said simply.

Her mother had heard from an old friend back near Maple Falls about Annie's "old boyfriend" who had died in that awful car crash. Denise Johnson had never regretted moving. The hospital in Minnesota did an excellent job on the surgeries and treatment, her husband was happier in his work, and her daughter graduated magna cum laude with an MBA from the university.

She had known Annie was not meant to be with the construction boy who wore holey jeans and wrote silly notes. She was somewhat relieved when she found out that there was no possible chance for Annie to return to him, for every once in a while her daughter had hinted at returning to Maple Falls.

The news hit Annie as though a brick had flown into her stomach. She felt a huge wave of nausea when her mother casually mentioned the car crash at dinner that night. Excusing herself from the rest of the dinner, she returned to her small apartment a couple blocks away from her parents' place. There she took out every note, every letter Shaun had written, until she found the last one he had left on her doorstep with the dried rose. She cried until she made herself sick and wrote a letter to his family, cursing herself furiously for not taking hold of her life sooner.

After walking in a haze of disbelief for over a month, she received a short note without a return address that informed her anonymously that Jerry had died two years ago, shortly after the accident, and that the Murrays had moved. Annie simply wept for them more.

It jolted her out of the cookie-cutter life her mother had fashioned for "her own good." It was time. Annie informed her parents that she was moving to North Carolina, to a city just about an hour away from the beloved small town of Maple Falls.

"You can't move."

"I can," said Annie, cutting her steak calmly and wondering why she hadn't felt the confidence to do this years before. She was an adult, capable of making her own decisions.

"But your job," Denise stuttered, looking at her husband, who looked as baffled as she did.

"You were climbing the ladder," he joined in. "You were right on track."

She laughed, although it didn't feel funny. "What track? Not mine. This has never been my dream. It was yours for me." Her parents stared at her, anger beginning to color the shock on their faces. "Don't you think we know how to make it? How to be a success? What's waiting for you in North Carolina? You'll be ruining it all, Annie, and for what? Shaun is gone now. There's no reason to move."

At that, Annie placed her silverware next to her plate, stood up with all the serenity she could muster, and pushed her chair in. Her voice shook, but she spoke with complete clarity. "I thought the worst thing was having to choose between my family and a man I loved. But what I am realizing, far too late, is that he loved me in a more real and genuine way than you are capable of. The worst thing is knowing he is gone, and I can never get him back."

Her mother stood up and faced her. "Don't you disrespect the life we gave you."

Annie pulled her purse onto her shoulder and sighed as she opened the door into the night, which felt refreshingly chill against her hot cheeks. "I need to do life on my own terms now."

One year later, she started a travel company and named it Compass Rose.

Though she lived near Maple Falls, she couldn't even bring herself to drive through the old town, afraid of the memories and heartache it would spur. However, immersed in her work, she finally started traveling to the places she'd dreamed of going for years but had always had excuses not to. She bought a house with a big yard and enough space to start a garden. Her parents begrudgingly visited her, and seeing her travel business in person softened a bit of their edges, pride breaking through their own stubbornness.

She explained to Shaun how all of it came to be, and he in turn shared his half of the story. Her mind reeled as he told her about the car accident, Jerry's heart attack, his move, Olivia, and Marie. One hand on her heart as she felt the rollercoaster of all that had happened with him, she unconsciously reached out for his hand and squeezed it. The touch alone sent waves of electricity through both of them, freezing them in their tracks. He'd ached for that simple gesture from her for so many years, and she from him. They stared at each other, until Annie broke the silence.

"It's like you're this whole new person …"

He nodded. "And you," he answered, gesturing around.

"But …" she started, then stopped.

"It's like no time has passed?" Shaun asked, with a hint of a question, letting her know he felt the same.

She nodded this time. "Being around you still feels like what it was like. Then."

His eyes smiled. "You feel like you, too."

As they talked, they skimmed the surface of every important issue, rushing to get out the crucial details of the last ten years that had brought them crashing together after so long.

Marie walked around the shop as they struggled to get a hold of the situation. While the grown-up conversation was interesting for a time, the trinkets and books soon drew Marie's attention. She picked up different pictures, gazing at them and looking up at large, beautiful posters. She grinned at the ones of tropical islands and Scotland, thinking of her dreams. Shaun had said she could walk around the bookshelves and table space, but to stay where he could see her. Marie didn't know why, but this made the woman look like she was about to cry. Annie realized as she watched him that she had been right all those years ago; she thought he would be a great dad.

He called Marie over at one point to ask her questions about the letter.

"I saw Mommy put it in the box, and it looked like she was hiding it from you," Marie said, grimacing a little bit. She didn't know which was worse, spying on her mom or not telling her dad sooner. He didn't look mad, but his eyebrows had stayed furrowed for a while. "So one day when she was napping, I pulled it out and read some of the words that I could."

Shaun nodded, pride not entirely hidden in his eyes. "Smart girl," he said. "Did you know Annie would be here?"

Marie shook her head, and her thick brown hair fell from shoulder to shoulder. "I didn't know what we'd find. I just knew it'd be something special."

"Because it was named Compass Rose? It's a part of the roses?" Annie asked gently.

Marie smiled shyly at her and nodded. "They're magic. And I thought if the person who wrote the letter knew about the roses, she might know the magic too. But I didn't know you'd be right here waiting." She shrugged knowingly. "Just kind of proves the magic, huh, Dad?" Still shy in front of Annie, Marie held onto Shaun's hand as her body wriggled around, wanting to explore the rest of the store. She scooted off when Annie pointed out the huge globe in the corner of the building, and the two adults watched her in silence for a couple of minutes.

"I can't believe you have a little girl," said Annie.

Shaun smiled. "Me either." Unsure how to bring it up, he quietly asked, "Do you? Have kids, that is?"

Annie shook her head, but didn't say much more yet, continuing to watch Marie as the thoughts spun in circles in her head—what to share, what to say, what to ask.

Shaun took his eyes off of Marie and looked directly at Annie, amazed at how good it felt just to be standing with her again, despite the gap of nearly a decade separating them. He wanted to hear more about her life, to fill in some of that empty space. He wished they could have that time back. He wanted to sit down and hear every detail about every minute they had been apart, swapping stories and sharing themselves as though they had just been on a long trip.

Marie wandered up to them with two glossy books, one of photos from around the world, and one, a traveler's guide. "Can I check these out? I have my library card," she asked Annie politely.

Annie and Shaun both laughed heartily, and Marie smiled unsurely back. Shaun started to pull out his wallet, saying, "It is your birthday after all, and this is where you wanted to come."

Annie knelt down to be on Marie's level. "They're yours," she said with a grin, nodding at the books. "My treat." Marie hugged them to her chest, and Annie asked, "You seem like a pretty awesome adventurer. Are you planning a trip somewhere?"

Marie squinted, thinking hard. "I want to go somewhere; I just haven't decided where my dad and I should go first."

Knowingly, Annie nodded. "It's hard to choose from so many places."

"Have you been anywhere?" Marie questioned quietly.

Gesturing around the little agency, Annie answered, "Well, it would be hard to tell so many people to go places if I didn't go to some really cool spots myself. I'm really lucky," she explained. "My whole job is to help people live their most fabulous, adventuresome dream. I help them pick a place to go and research the neat things to do there. I have this little shop for things they might need. I pick out their airplane and places to stay. Then I get to hear about how awesome it was. So I kind of want to go on a few myself here and there, just to see what they are talking about."

"Have you been to Scotland?" Marie asked.

"Not yet, but it's always been on the list. I heard it's really special," Annie said, glancing sideways at Shaun. "Last year, I went to some warm places called Peru and

126

Argentina. I saw a lot of llamas and some whales and went up the highest stairs ever to the top of a mountain."

She led Marie to a wall that had pictures of her customers, all in different places around the world. On top of icy mountains, in front of the Eiffel Tower, floating in a gondola, on the Great Wall of China. Marie gasped and pointed, spotting a few pictures of Annie in them. They were smaller pictures, with a white background framing it, and writing beneath the picture.

"That's called a polaroid," Shaun explained as Marie touched it. "It pops out of your camera as soon as you take it, and then the picture appears."

"Cool," breathed Marie. "Where is this?"

Annie squatted down to see. "Ah, that's in Costa Rica with my best friend, Zoe." Annie smiled sideways at Shaun, whose eyes widened in recognition. "You know Zoe is always down for a trip."

Looking back at Marie, Annie continued, "We're on a zipline there through the jungle. They hook you up, and you go zooming through the treetops. It's a little bit terrifying, but mostly it's wildly fun."

Marie giggled. "Dad, let's do that!"

Shaun smiled a little wistfully.

Annie glanced at her watch. "Well, we can't go there, but maybe I can give you a little taste? Do you have time for a quick adventure?

Chapter 20

Annie's heart leapt a bit as she led Shaun and Marie out of the shop, locked up, and headed down the street and across a busy intersection. "This is a park," she explained as the sidewalk brought them to a wide entrance. "But it's got a hidden gem in it."

She wound them around fountains and gathered trees with benches underneath, over stone bridges with cheerful streams of water, until they came to a large building made mostly of glass. She gestured them inside, and Shaun's arm brushed against hers, stopping her heart as though she was a teenager again. She took a deep breath and stepped in.

"Woah," said Marie, her head craned back, staring up and around.

"It's a conservatory," Shaun caught on, smiling.

They followed the path through the warm air, lush green plants surrounding them with life. There were full trees indoors, mossy rocks and flowers of every color, even a stream that laughed its way through the beautiful space. Marie squeaked as a bird flew directly in front of them, swooping into a large bush on the other side. She counted six brightly colored fish in a pond, three frogs, ten weird-looking bugs, four butterflies, and countless colorful, chirping birds. Annie pointed to a spiral staircase that led to a treehouse-like boardwalk where, Marie delightedly realized, they could explore the upper level of the canopy.

"It's no zipline," Annie said. "But it's still one of my favorite adventures in town."

"I love it here," agreed Marie, leaning up against Shaun.

"Hold that thought," Annie said, reaching into her enormous bag she used as a purse. A wave of nostalgia hit Shaun as he remembered teasing her about always carrying one that size and being prepared for any and all situations that could arise. Today, she pulled out a polaroid camera and, directing it at the dad-daughter pair, told them, "Smile, guys."

Right as she took the picture, a blue butterfly floated by and landed on Marie's arm, the pure delight captured as the camera flashed. Shaun showed Marie how to wave the photo back and forth until their images appeared.

"This is AMAZING!" Marie yelled, unable to contain her excitement, holding onto the photo. "Can we keep it?"

"Absolutely," Annie answered as they continued on. As Marie bounced from area to area, enthralled with every different corner of the conservatory, Shaun and Annie strolled slowly behind her, suddenly a bit shy to be so close. "So you and Marie grow roses?" Annie asked quietly.

He scratched the scruff on his neck. There was so much to talk about. There was so much to face. After years and years of building a wall to his past, it was all crashing down around him, and he was looking at the mess of himself he had left behind, trying to bring it into the new person he had become, along with the daughter who skipped joyfully in front of them.

"Annie, I'm kind of freaking out right now," he said simply, ignoring her question.

Her head turned toward him, a piece of her hair falling out of place, reminding him of how it did the same thing so many years ago. She brushed it impatiently back. "I mean

… I don't know what to do with this either, Shaun." Her voice was lined with apprehension once more. She was confused, thrilled, frustrated, scared, on an emotional roller coaster. But strangely enough, Annie felt the familiar homelike comfort she had always known with the Murrays—that had not changed, even after so long. No one had given her that feeling since then, or maybe she didn't let them. Either way, she dated men over the years but moved on when they were ready to settle down, much to the dismay of her mother. She wasn't going to settle for someone less. She wanted that feeling of calm and peace and the ability to just be unapologetically herself. She hadn't felt that fierce love that burned as strongly as it had for Shaun. She watched her friends fall in love, she went to their weddings, she brought plus-ones. But never did she try to catch that bouquet. After she moved back to North Carolina, it was easy to put off any serious dating while she traveled, got her business set up, and made friends in the town.

"Is there … is there someone you're with?" Shaun asked tentatively, seemingly reading her mind.

"Honestly," Annie replied, "I've really just been getting to know myself these past few years. I haven't been ready for anyone else for real just yet, you know?"

Shaun nodded. He seemed to hesitate, then stopped. His hand reached out for hers, and though he meant to just hold her hand for a moment, the feeling of her skin made him draw her toward him, like one of Marie's magnet trains that just pulled for its match. After hesitating a moment, their arms finally flew around each other in an embrace. Each clung to the other tightly, as though if they let go, they'd disappear again. Their foreheads touched, and she felt her stomach flip, still in shock. Tears welled as she realized he was truly here, alive, holding her again.

"I can't lose you again," he said in a low voice.

She thought about when they were together, all those years ago. She thought about Jerry, about how peaceful it was to garden with him. She thought of Charlotte and the rest of the family, and the long days she spent with them. She thought of the heartache when she believed Shaun had died, and how she finally took life into her own hands. She thought of the small garden plot she had started the week after she bought a house with a yard, knowing she was ready for a home she'd always dreamed of. She looked at the man in front of her for a long time, his words echoing in her head. Finally, she answered, "Shaun, you never did."

Chapter 21

The magnolia trees were still there. He had walked the two miles from the bus stop, passing buildings he was sure he had forgotten but had brought him right back as soon as he saw them. There were some new houses, new traffic lights, new businesses—all of which unnerved him. He had been gone eight years. Eight long years.

The house thankfully looked exactly the same. He was relieved for that. Bringing his hand up to knock on the familiar, heavy wooden door, he felt sick with absolute nervousness. He subconsciously held his breath, his knees even shaking. Deciding he couldn't knock on his own home's door, he tried the doorknob. It turned easily, and he stepped inside as quietly as possible.

The sight of the foyer made his insides tighten as the smell of a previous life hit him like a wave. The hall was cozy as always, the staircase to his right and living room to the left. The furniture was the same soft gray, Charlotte's trinkets and accents providing pops of colors like they always had. The doorway that led to the kitchen was straight ahead, and he could see the familiar tile on the floor. Again, he was shocked at how long he had been gone. He could hear someone moving inside and was paralyzed with apprehension.

"Brady?" a familiar voice called, and Shaun heard the stove creak open. "What are you doing stopping by now?" Charlotte was smiling and wiping her hands on a dish towel as she bustled into the hallway where Shaun was still standing. "How was—" She froze, the towel hanging from one of her hands dropped to the floor. Her eyes were wide, and her jaw fell.

Shaun simply stood with his hands by his side, looking back at her, his face pulled tightly.

Charlotte crossed the distance between them in two strides and grabbed him into a tight embrace as though she would not let go. He finally let out his breath as he held onto her just as closely, the feel of his mother's hug sparking another huge wave of memories.

"You're home," she said, tears pouring down her face. "Oh, you're home. I was so afraid you weren't coming back, Shaun. So afraid." She took his face in her hands, examining every inch of him.

"Ma ... I've got ... I've got a lot to explain ..." he choked out, doing his best to rein in the huge array of emotions he was feeling.

"Yes, you sure do, Shaun Murray," she said, the tears still coming. "I have half a mind to wring your neck right now. Eight years you were gone. I lost your father, and then I lost you, damnit."

He nodded solemnly, wondering how he would ever explain now that he was here. She lifted his chin up, a smile breaking through her tear-streaked face.

"I'm sure you've gone through some things that have changed you a great deal, and you'll have a lot to share. We've got some things to talk about, but, Shaun ..." She held his chin still.

He met her eyes.

"I'm glad you're home."

Upon Charlotte's request, they headed to the backyard to sit on the patio. He balked internally when he saw how few rose bushes were left. The trees and bushes they had planted had grown a great deal, and Charlotte had kept the yard full of different flowers, but there were only five or six rose bushes along the fence line. He gazed around at his surroundings as though he was in a bubble. Charlotte sat down in a chair, letting him take in the changes.

"It's just me here," she answered his unspoken question softly, and he nodded, selfishly relieved and amazed that his mom could still read him.

The furniture was different, but from its weathered look, Shaun supposed they had owned it for a good while. The picnic table to the side needed to be painted again. It was a navy blue now; it had been a fresh white when Shaun had left. The waist-high brick walls that surrounded the patio were completely covered in ivy. One of the maple trees provided a lot more shade than he remembered. He felt Charlotte's soft hand pulling his own to sit beside her. "I'm sorry I didn't visit," he said suddenly and quietly. He had spoken so little; his voice sounded strange to him.

She shrugged neutrally. "You were running. Trying to sever any ties with what happened that summer and fall. I won't lie, Shaun. I was furious with you, and it took all my self-control to not chase you. I ached for you to come home, for you to heal. I'm a mother. It's what we do."

Shaun leaned back in his chair. "Not all mothers are as good as you, Ma."

"Oh?" Charlotte said, raising her eyebrows. She caught the opportunity to take her son in as he looked around the yard, sorting through his many thoughts. There was no doubt that he had matured a great deal. His hair was the same strawberry blond as her own, although he still lacked the gray. His face was less youthful, hardened and grown. She felt the roughness of his hand, which she held in her own, and tried to read the weight he carried in his big, blue eyes. She found it hard to believe he was past thirty. His chest rose to speak, and she waited patiently for him.

"My daughter does not have a mother like you."

The air went still around them, and she stared at him, her mouth in a surprised "O." He was gazing at the leftover rose bushes. He knew that a thousand questions were racing through his mother's mind. He pulled out the wooden box he had brought with him, handing it to Charlotte, who wordlessly opened it and pulled out photo after photo of Marie from the day she was born all the way to her first day of kindergarten. Tears streaming down her face, she touched Marie's face in a picture of her swinging, smiling so wide her eyes were shut.

"I'm not married," Shaun answered simply as his mom slowly turned through each photo, not missing one. He stared at the rose bushes, seeing the memory of his dad working so steadily there years ago. "But I have a six-year-old girl. Her name is Marie. Her mom, Olivia, Marie, and I live in a little house up north. I've wanted to come here with her so many times, but once time passed after she was born, I just didn't know how. I didn't know how to announce her and my life. And now, I'm here because ..." He paused. Why was he here? He paused, and Charlotte squeezed his hand, the shock still clearly written on her face but the reassurance firm in his palm.

"Well, the truth of it is, I just found out Olivia, my daughter's mother, has also been hiding from a past she feared and hid a letter Annie wrote seven years ago. I knew nothing about it until Marie and I ran into Annie two days ago. And, well, it all came back. Annie. Dad. Everything."

Shaun didn't think it was possible, but Charlotte's eyes widened further. "Oh, Shaun," she whispered.

He pulled his hand away and put his forehead in his palm, leaning on the arm of the chair, struggling to keep himself together. "I'm sorry, Ma. I was too ashamed to reach out after so long. I couldn't bear to disappoint you more."

Charlotte ran her hands through her wavy, now mostly gray, hair. Perhaps she had adopted some of Jerry's serenity.

"That's no excuse," she said bluntly. "You couldn't bear to disappoint yourself more, Shaun, and that's why you stayed gone."

He looked up and met her eyes. Her face softened for a moment.

"Tell me about my granddaughter."

Shaun's face broke into a true smile, and Charlotte found a strange sense of relief. It wasn't a huge smile, but it was real.

"Her name is Marie Charlotte Murray," he said quietly. Charlotte's hand went to her mouth, the other to her heart, as her eyes welled.

"I stayed at home a lot with her in her younger years while Olivia worked. She's in kindergarten now, though. I help her with her homework, and Ma, she's so smart." His voice was traced with fierce pride as he went on. "She struggles with some things in school but catches on right away if you take the time to explain it. She's so creative and just loves stories. We started … we started a rose garden this March." The words came out thickly as Charlotte watched him describe what appeared to be the only light in his life, her eyes still brimming.

"She loves it; she loves the garden. Dad would have a field day with her." He laughed to himself. "Teaching her about beetles, the black spot, how to prune …"

"But you do," cut in Charlotte. "You teach her?"

Shaun brought his gaze back to his mother. "I do. I thought my life was over when Olivia said she was pregnant. We'd been dating for two months, and she was not the woman I wanted to be with for the rest of my life."

Charlotte closed her eyes and opened them when Shaun started speaking again.

"But Ma … when she was born … she was so tiny … so beautiful. And she was mine. I left here looking for myself, and instead I found Marie. She was a miracle to me."

Charlotte listened to him talk, letting the sound of his voice roll through her mind, at first just thankful to be hearing it again. Shaun explained why he and Olivia stayed together at first, how hard she was to live with, how he hated raising Marie in that environment, and what little choice he felt like he had. He told her about Marie, her first words, her questions and curiosity. He told her about the rose that bloomed right outside the hospital window the day she was born.

As he spoke, he processed what had happened between he and Annie, much of which Charlotte already knew. All those years ago, when Annie did not come back to him after moving, he gave up hope. He had only just realized that in running from the memory of losing her and then his father, he was never able to get past the losses that broke his heart. So he spent his fatherhood crushed that he was not doing half the job his father and mother had done in raising a family, while the other part of his heart denied the ache for Annie that had never left.

"I realized I messed up, Ma," he said, holding her hand still. "I want to set it right."

Charlotte smiled at the heroic nature of his words. He had a lot to figure out, a lot of catching up to do, and a lot of rebuilding if he could face it. "So what will you do?"

He smiled at her, feeling the fog lift ever so slightly. "I think it's time to fix it."

Chapter 22

"Strawberry please," Marie said, as she sat in the ice cream booth.

There had been a lot of trips, and a lot of grown-up talks. She was ready to know exactly what was going on.

"Did you do okay with Mom while I was gone?" Shaun asked as they sat down with their milkshakes, whipped cream, and rainbow sprinkles.

Marie nodded. Her mom had seemed different. Less mad. A little nervous. She actually let Marie play dress up, and even spread out a towel on the bathroom floor where they sat criss-cross applesauce and did makeup on each other's faces. "You're really pretty," Marie had told her as she looped the blush brush around Olivia's cheeks and nose. Marie knew that her mom would have to go back to work and probably get cranky again, but she wanted to make it last as long as she could.

Even more, Marie wanted to know more about what everything meant once the roses led to Annie, but Shaun had said on the bus ride home that she had done an amazing job following the roses, and now he had to figure some things out and would explain as much as he could at their ice cream date.

"Where did you go?" Marie asked, never hesitating with questions.

Shaun took a deep breath, leaning backward in the booth. "After we saw Annie, I went to see your grandma in Maple Falls," he said. "My mom."

Marie's mouth dropped. She didn't even know what question to ask next.

"I should have gone to visit her a long time ago, but I had a lot of feelings about it," Shaun said, trying to pick his words carefully. "I was really sad when my dad died. But I didn't want to think about being sad, so I decided to move away. It was really kind of selfish of me," Shaun went on, Marie listening with a surprising attention span. "So I had to tell my ma I was sorry for doing that and that I missed her."

Marie continued to eat her milkshake, processing while trying to imagine what her grandma looked like.

Shaun reached out for her hand and squeezed it like he always did to pass on a little love. "But most importantly, I got to show her pictures of you and tell her how special you are."

At this, Marie's heart leapt. "What does she look like, Dad?"

"Well I don't know if I could do her justice." He nudged her arm with eyebrows raised. "Why don't we go see her for yourself? She really, really wants to meet you, and there's some other people in our family who probably want to meet you too."

Marie shoved her milkshake aside. "Today? Are we going today?"

Laughing, Shaun answered that it might be a few days. "There's some more stuff I want to get your thoughts on. You're a smart kid, and you pick up on a lot. And over the years, you may have picked up on the fact that your mom and I fight sometimes. We don't always agree on everything." At Marie's downcast nod, Shaun continued, "We had a big, long talk about that. About how we can be nicer to each other and be more like a team. But even though we want to be a good parent team for you, we might do that living in different houses. We love you, and you'll still have both of us in your life. So, while some things for mommy and daddy's relationship will change, loving *you* will not change. Does that make sense?"

Marie absently tore her napkin into little pieces. "Whose house will I live in?" she asked tentatively.

Shaun answered, "You can always tell us what you want, and we'll do our best to make it happen. But right now, we're thinking you'd live with Daddy and visit Mom some weekends."

Marie broke into a grin. "Will it be our house? With our rose garden?" she asked, the questions flowing more easily now.

Scratching at his beard, Shaun mulled how to approach this. "You know where we went to that cool conservatory with the bird and trees? I might be looking for a job near there. What do you think about that? It's a little far away, but I think if we go together, it could be really fun. And we can bring our roses. Even plant some new ones."

"Will Mom stay here?"

Shaun shook his head. "Mom's ready for a new adventure too. She'll be close enough that it won't be too far for your weekends with her. You'll still have both of us."

Stirring the remains of her milkshake, she took in this new information, finally nodding as if offering official approval. "I'm okay with that," she voiced, making Shaun laugh, tinged with some very tangible relief.

"Will we see Annie?" Marie pressed. It was the one thing she hadn't asked her dad about but was dying to know.

"Do you want to see Annie?"

Marie nodded. "I like her," she answered. "Don't you?"

Shaun, unable to hide his heart from his daughter, answered, "I do. Aside from my number one girl." He brushed Marie's nose. "I've loved Annie a long time."

140

Marie giggled, spooning strawberry milkshake into her mouth. "Gross, Dad!" she laughed. But really, she knew it. And it made her happy.

He sighed, watching her. "Marie, you're a special kiddo, sweetheart. Your dad has been struggling to figure some stuff out for years, and here you are, six years old, smart enough to follow the roses and lead us to treasure."

She grinned. "Six and a half," she corrected. "And it was easy. Grandad's roses are everywhere."

Chapter 23

Olivia thought she would feel more resentment. She thought she would feel more fear. Knowing that Shaun knew about Annie, knowing that Annie knew about Shaun. Knowing that there was no keeping them apart now. After telling Shaun her whole story, she was worried he would leave, take Marie, and never look back.

But when he came home from seeing his mom, he brought her something. An envelope with a rose laid on top of it. He put it on the table in front of her after Marie went to bed and beckoned for her to come sit. She was tense, waiting for him to break the news. She swore she wouldn't go back to her dad's, no matter how hard things got. She had started researching apartments that she could maybe afford on her waitressing check, people who needed roommates. Everything in the city was so expensive, and she was reminded why she and Shaun decided to stay together in the first place.

Olivia sat down across from him, waiting to speak until he did.

He reached out for her hand, and she let him take it, feeling the warmth seep into her own.

"I'm sorry we weren't honest with each other for so long," he finally said simply.

Olivia nodded.

"We aren't the right people for each other," he whispered, and she nodded again. "We haven't been for a long time. We knew that. It hasn't been good." Simple sentences. Simple facts. She took simple breaths, steeling herself for the hardships that lay ahead on her own. No simple answers. But she'd made it before, she could do it again. She didn't know how she'd do her share for Marie, but she could try.

"I'd like to move. With Marie," he said, concern etched across his face. Panic flashed across hers.

"Hear me out," he replied to her tension, taking a deep breath and continuing to hold her hand in his. "Part of our problem was that you felt trapped by parenting and our unhealthy relationship. I think it might help for me to have full custody of Marie, with you seeing her for whatever time you can every week, or every other. I think you'll be able to be a better mom to her when you are able to give yourself time to find what it is you want."

Olivia stared him, unsure of how to respond. *A better mom. What it is you want.* A tiny flame of hope flickered in her chest, a feeling she wasn't sure whether to trust or not.

Gesturing at the envelope, Shaun said quietly, "Open it."

She pulled out two things: one that made her eyes widen, and another that made them close to keep back tears. A check, and a printed photo of her holding Marie as a baby, sleeping with Marie on her chest and her own arm draped protectively around Marie's tiny swaddled body.

"You made the choice to give us this daughter," Shaun said earnestly. "This amazing, beautiful, smart daughter. You took care of her even when it made your life harder." He pointed at the photo. "I believe you can be a good mom to her."

She traced the edges of the picture, remembering. She slid the check back across the table. "I'm not going to take your money, Shaun."

"I want you to move near us."

She stared at him.

"You don't have to," he said quickly. "I think you know my heart is with Annie, and I'd like to be close to my mom and brothers and sisters again. But that doesn't mean I'm going to ditch you and leave you high and dry. I don't want you to ever have to go back to your father; I don't want you to feel like you're alone. I'm grateful that you brought Marie into my world, and I want to make this work in whatever ways we can. Even though we aren't together, I think we can still be a team together; we can still be there for Marie together. Maybe in a healthier way now that we aren't resenting each other so much."

Blinking back tears, Olivia answered, "This is the most we've ever talked."

He smiled. "There's a restaurant manager position open in a town like forty-five minutes from where I'm hoping to move. It pays good. Housing is affordable. It had a cool vibe from what I saw. I wonder if you'd want to try it?"

Try it. Try a new city. A new plan. Looking at the photo and the check written out in Shaun's messy scrawl, Olivia felt a sense of safety she had never felt, even when they were technically together. She had expected when the door closed with Shaun, that it would slam shut. But somehow, it felt like the right door had finally opened. Even free from the relationship with Shaun, she had a family that wasn't going to leave her, that would support her trying to become something. She could be there for them too, as they found their own paths to peace. Her eyes crinkled into the half-moons Shaun had seen so rarely. A smile finally broke across her face.

"Yeah," she said. "I'm in."

Chapter 24

Every night since they had walked into Compass Rose, her phone rang at exactly 9:30 p.m. "Hey," he'd whisper softly. She knew he was on the patio outside. She knew Marie was asleep by then. She knew it was their time. Annie still pressed the phone against her ear, her heart clenching at the proof that Shaun was on the other end.

They'd share bits and pieces about their day, their jobs, their updates. Soon, he asked if he could visit her again.

"A visit doesn't feel like enough," she said, craving time with him. When he half-joked that they could move tomorrow, she said, "I wish you could."

"I haven't thought about much else, honestly. But I want to know what you think. Is it too soon? Is it too much? I mean, it's not just me now; I've got Marie," he questioned sincerely. "I would, Annie. Now that I know you're there, all I want to do is get in the car and drive back to you. But I understand if it's too soon, and you need to think about if you're ready or not."

She laughed. "Too soon? It's been ten years too long."

She knew they couldn't pick right back up where they started. She knew they had changed and grown and become more than they were fresh out of college. She knew Shaun's first priority was his daughter, as it should be. She knew he wanted to support Olivia becoming independent. She knew it was complicated. But she was not making the same mistake twice. She would do whatever it took. When she talked to Zoe on the phone earlier, one of the only friends who truly understood how her world had just turned upside down, Zoe told her, "I knew it. I knew you two were meant to be together, and damn it if he doesn't rise from the dead ten years later. Girl, you better not let him go this time."

"Do you think it'll be okay to start such a serious relationship so fast with Marie in the picture?" Annie had wondered out loud.

Zoe was blunt as always. "Are you ready for a straight up family? Because you'll become a second mama pretty quickly to this little girl."

It didn't take Annie more than a second to answer. "I'm in. I've thought pretty hard about it. I just hope they'll want me in their family."

When Shaun told her with no question in his voice that he wanted to be where she was, back near Maple Falls, she breathed a sigh of relief.

"Really?" Annie half-whispered back to him.

"Can I come there this weekend, and we can talk more about it? Just us? I'll have Olivia stay with Marie so we can talk more."

And they did. They talked about what they could do. They looked at apartments that might work for him and Marie, but she also pulled open the guest room in her house and pointed out how they could decorate it for Marie—make it hers one day. They looked up every job opening that had a chance. They called Charlotte and talked with her, Shaun making plans to bring Marie there the next week. They talked about trips—where they could go together, where they could take Marie. She introduced to him to her friends at the local café where she frequented often. They weaved through Annie's garden, sometimes talking, sometimes not. They lay together in her bed, sometimes talking, sometimes not, sometimes moving slowly together as they learned how to love each other again. They watched old movies together, and cooked together, and slept, getting used to the way each other breathed at night.

Before he ducked into his car to head back, he kissed her slowly. As he pulled away, he held her chin. "You're sure you're ready for this?"

"I've never been so sure of anything," she whispered back. "You come back, Shaun Murray, and let's get our life started together."

Chapter 25

Their car pulled into the driveway, and he and Marie stepped out. Marie ogled at the white house with the bright green door, built on a gently sloping hill on a quaint street of beautiful old houses. An old station wagon was parked in front, and flowers were painted on the mailbox, just like Annie had said. He walked up the sidewalk, giving Marie's hand an extra squeeze. Two weeks had passed since they had taken that trip to Compass Rose, and now here they were.

"Hey, Daddy, I think there's a party out there," Marie cut in, pointing toward the back.

Shaun led them to the gate and opened it, stepping into the backyard. As he looked around, a wave of surprise and every emotion hit him.

His sister, Liza, now in her mid-twenties and very pregnant, was waddling to embrace him as fast as her size would allow. He felt her arms fly around his neck and felt the bulge of her stomach against his.

"Oh my god, Shaun," she cried, holding onto him as best she could. "When Annie called the other week to invite us here to see you, I just about cried for twenty-four hours. I can't believe it; I just can't believe it. I've missed you!"

In a daze, he hugged her back, half laughing and half crying, holding on tightly to Marie's hand. "There's two of you," he said, gesturing at her belly. "Ma told me when I saw her; I'm so happy for you, Liza."

Brady, about a foot taller than he had been the last time Shaun saw him, was striding across the lawn. "Shaun! It's about time, man!" He was yelling, and before Shaun knew it, he was also wrapped around him, patting him heartily on the back as Liza wiped away her tears and beckoned for a tall dark man to come over to finally meet his brother-in-law. Billy had driven in, his hair shorter, his beard longer, but underneath was the same face. He simultaneously shook his head and grinned at his brother.

As Billy and Shaun clapped each other's back in a brotherly embrace, Shaun said, "I'm sorry. I really let everyone down by leaving for so long."

"We all need some space sometimes." Billy shrugged. "Knew you'd come around. Didn't think it'd take so damn long, but knew you'd come back to us."

Marie scooted behind Shaun's leg shyly, looking up at her father for guidance. He scooped her up into his arms, holding her small body as her little arms wrapped around his shoulders.

Shaun took a deep breath. "Everyone, this is my daughter, Marie." He looked at Marie with a reassuring grin and brushed some dirt off of her face. "Marie, sweetie, this is our family I told you about. These are all your uncles and aunts."

Marie nodded, eyes wide, and smiled bashfully at the group who was staring at her. She felt her heart skip a couple beats as she looked around at the group. Her father's family. Her family. Marie was thrilled and squeezed more tightly around her father's neck.

She had known some things would change. Both her parents had sat her down to talk more about the plans, reassuring her they would always be supporting each other, even though they weren't together. Having lived under the stress of their tension and bitterness, Marie felt relief that they had a plan to change things. Though she was sad about missing her friends at school, moving was also a welcome adventure. Marie was so excited to finally meet her grandma when they moved near Maple Falls, but she had no idea she had a whole family waiting for her.

Shaun pointed as his mother came bustling out with Annie, carrying large trays of food to set on the picnic table they had set up in the large yard. Charlotte looked over at all the commotion and set the tray down hurriedly.

"Everybody's here?" Shaun asked her as she came in for a huge warm hug, smelling of food and the perfume she always wore. "I thought we were coming to see you tomorrow!"

"Annie called us all up." Charlotte's face was flushed with excitement, and she teared up when she looked at Shaun holding Marie. "Oh my word, oh my word. Is this my grandbaby? Is this sweet Marie?"

Marie looked up at Shaun expectantly, grinning, and he nodded down at her. "That's your grandma," he said.

Charlotte scooped her out of his arms and hugged her tight. "You are absolutely beautiful!" she cried happily. "Look at you! Come help me cook, love! And tell me all about your school and what you and your daddy do in the garden!" Marie looked back at Shaun for approval once more before he nodded. "Tell them what grade you're in," he said.

She looked back at Charlotte. "I'm about to finish kindergarten at Locke Elementary School. I rode the bus myself, and I got fifteen book points this year."

The group smiled widely; they wowed and treated her as any extended family should.

"Can I call you Grandma?" Marie asked, her eyes prickling a little bit and her heart feeling lots, as her dad liked to say.

Charlotte wrapped her into a warm hug. "Nothing would make me happier, Marie. I love, love, love that I get to be your grandma."

Shaun could barely stop smiling. *A lot of catching up to do indeed,* he thought, looking at Liza's expectant belly and watching Billy and Brady fill their plates on the table. Everybody had done a lot of living, and it was time to begin sharing again.

He looked around for Annie and spotted her setting out paper plates and laughing with Charlotte and Marie about something. She was wearing a loose sundress that fit the warm weather perfectly. She looked older, as did everyone, but she still had the same spirit in her eyes, was still the Annie he had always known.

He crossed the lawn and lifted her into a huge hug, whispering his thanks. She held on, then leaned back to smile at the happiness written across his face.

"We're all set, packing up our house," he said, and her green eyes widened. "Olivia and I talked with Marie, and she's actually excited about moving. Olivia is actually interviewing for a restaurant manager position about an hour away from here; she wants to be close to Marie for a few visits each month. This would be a good pay increase for her so she could stand on her own two feet. I want to help make sure she gets settled; the better she is doing, the better it is for Marie."

Nodding, Annie agreed. "Absolutely. That's all such great news."

Shaun's dimple deepened. "And my boss put in a good word for me with the main construction company here. I interview next week."

"Shaun, that's amazing," reveled Annie, her heart leaping with disbelief that this was really happening. "An interview already! Is it a project manager job like you've been doing?"

He grinned sideways at her. "A bit of a career shift actually. They are looking for an internal communication member. It's not the dreamiest of writing jobs, but I'd be working on marketing materials, reports, and outreach for local opportunities."

"You're doing this," said Annie. "All those years ago, when you'd tell me your plans ..."

"I'm doing what I should have done many years ago. A lot of things I should have done many years ago, actually." Shaun tucked Annie's head beneath his chin, a familiar and soothing contentment between them. He nodded toward her thriving rose garden. "Marie and I do need a place to move our five rose bushes though. They'll be needing a good home."

"Well," she said, "I think I've got the perfect place."

Hours later, the family was piled in every chair Annie owned, sitting around telling stories of the last years. During a lull in the conversation, Shaun excused himself and wandered off for a moment to let it all soak in, leaning against a fence that lined Annie's small garden. As he let the evening's nostalgia drift in, he breathed in the early summer air, heavy with grass and flowers from Annie's yard. *Dad would have loved this*, he thought to himself.

He patted his pocket where he held the box with the ring he had picked out so many years ago. Tonight wasn't the night though. They didn't know it yet, but six months later, they'd be on top of a mountain in Scotland, looking over a magical lake with Marie. That's when she would say yes, and Marie would throw flowers into the air like confetti.

He heard footsteps behind him and turned to see who it was. Marie was walking to him quietly.

"She must sing a lot of Beyoncé, Dad; those bushes are way bigger than ours," Marie observed as Shaun laughed. "Is Grandad in those roses, like at our house?" she asked.

The pang that usually hit his heart when his dad was mentioned felt less sharp. A sense of healing had wrapped around the wound in his heart, filling a hole that had been gaping, wide open, for so long. "He sure is. And if you look around at all these people here tonight, he's in all of them, too." He lifted Marie up into a hug and walked back toward the group of people waiting.

"All of them?" she asked.

"Each and every one. Even you."

"Even me?" Marie nuzzled her forehead against Shaun's, sleepy after the long day of excitement.

"Even you," he repeated as they looked out over the roses. "Don't you know, if you hold on to someone you love, you'll never lose them, no matter how hard you try? You just have to remember the things from the stories you love about Grandad, the things that make you smile, and he'll be there."

"Just like the roses," Marie added as Shaun smiled, hoisting her into another hug.

Annie glanced over to see Shaun and Marie by her garden, and the warmth of their dad-and-daughter relationship was palpable. She let her gaze wander to the family all around, friends she had missed so much in the last ten years, friends who had dropped everything to come welcome Shaun and his daughter. She felt the forgiveness, the relief, the coming to terms with the messiness of life, the bonds that withheld a storm … she felt all of it radiating in the family around her.

And she swore, for a moment, she saw a lean old man in black ironed slacks, a crisp white shirt, and fine polished shoes, with gray hair parted neatly on the side, walking through the garden. He had warm, pleasant eyes and a soft smile, pruning each bush ever so patiently so that every flower answered back with a full and mighty bloom. He nodded once before his shadow faded into the garden, leaving Annie to the merry chatter of the family and the soft evening breeze.

"What a gift," she said out loud as Shaun walked toward her. She was not sure who exactly she was talking to. But her gratitude rolled into the night, and the night replied with the grace and gentle movement of a flower on the verge of opening to its full and complete celebration of life.

END

ABOUT THE AUTHOR

Carly Eccles Sheaffer lives in Virginia with her husband, three wild but wonderful kids, a rescue dog who thinks it's a human, and a baby boy in the sky. Carly loves the power of stories—creating them, reading them, remembering them. When she's not teaching college writing, working on a book, or chasing around her little ones, Carly and her family enjoy DIY house projects, building sandcastles, exploring the mountains, and creating adventures together.